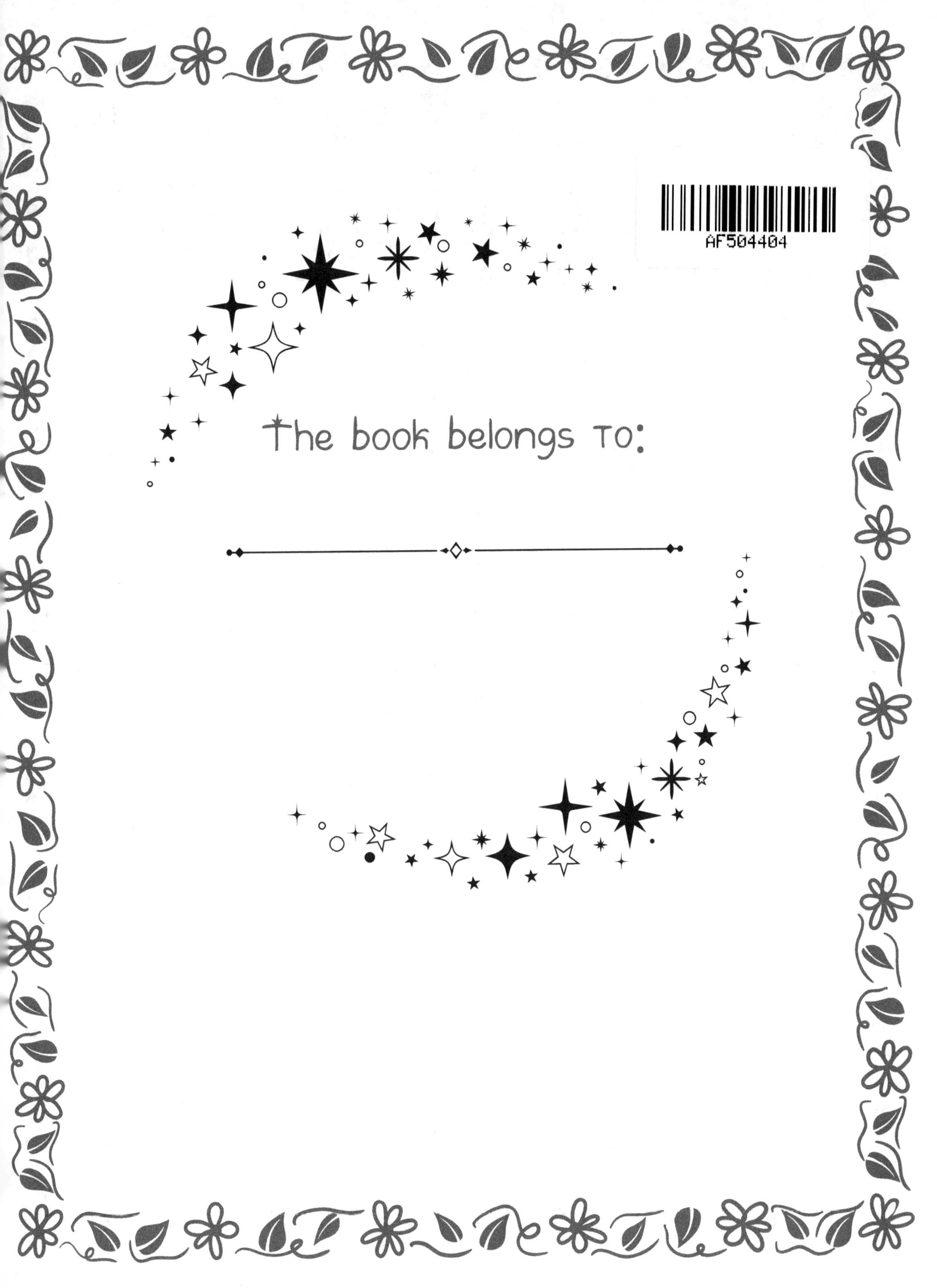
AF504404
the book belongs to:

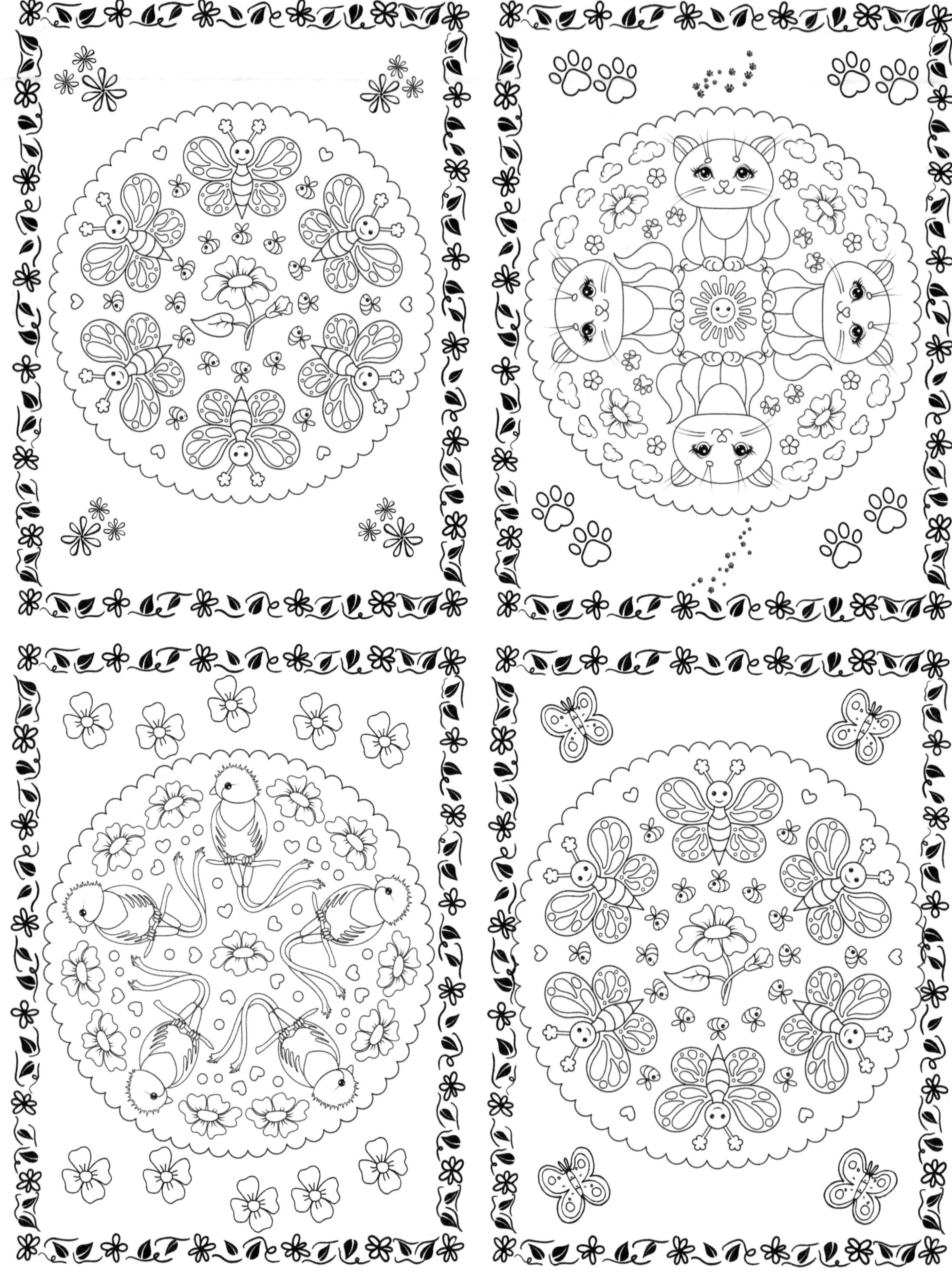

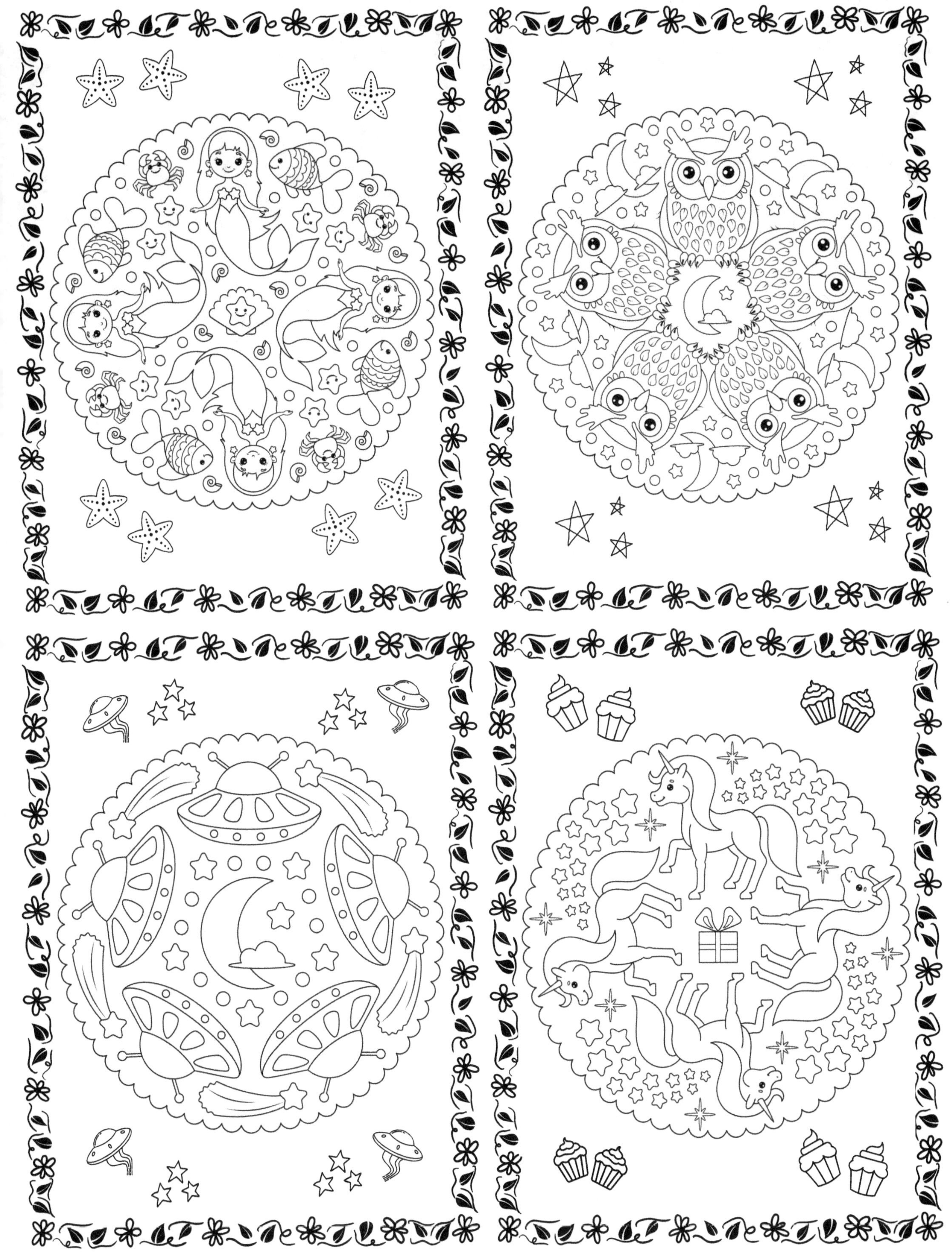

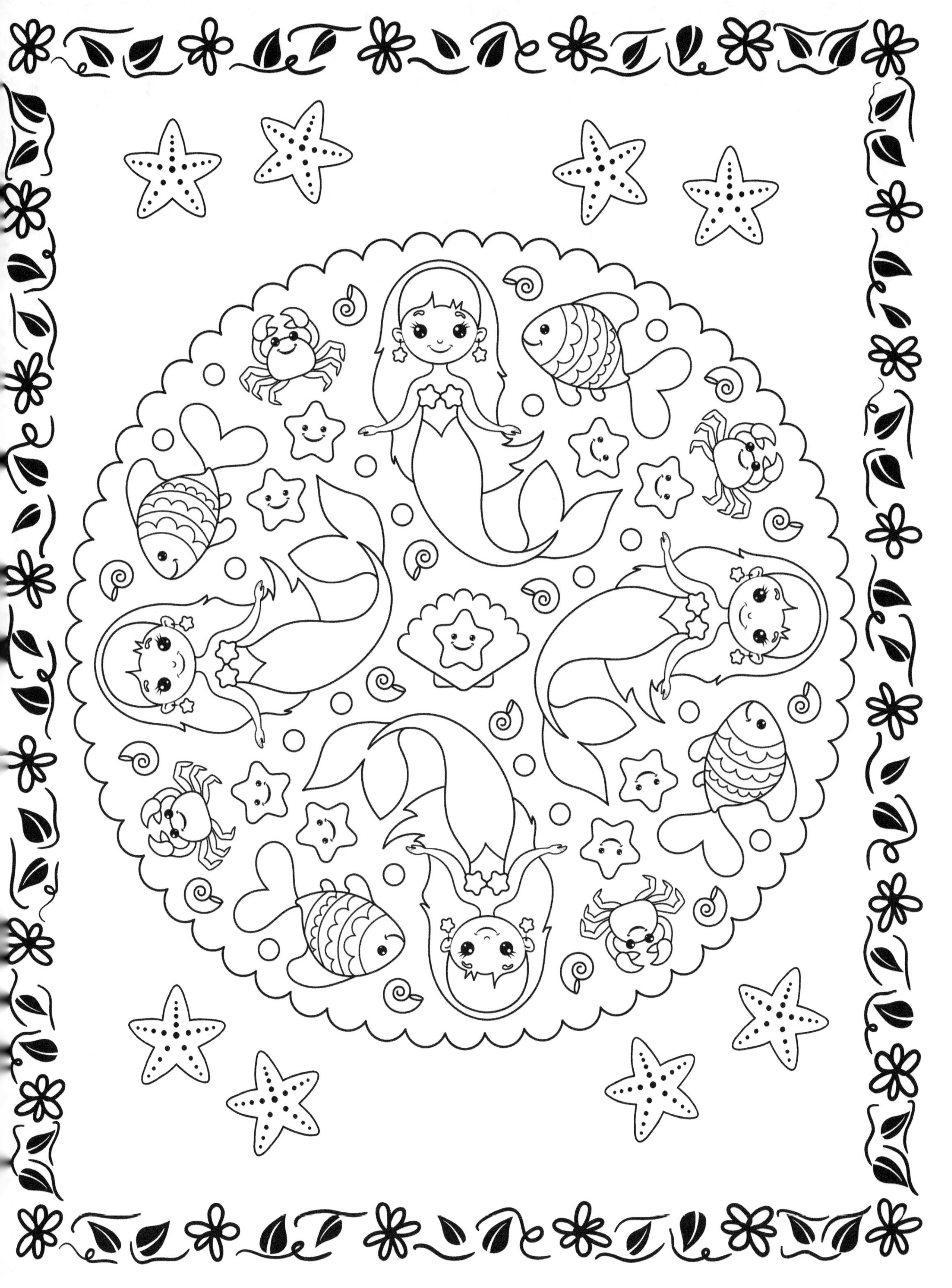

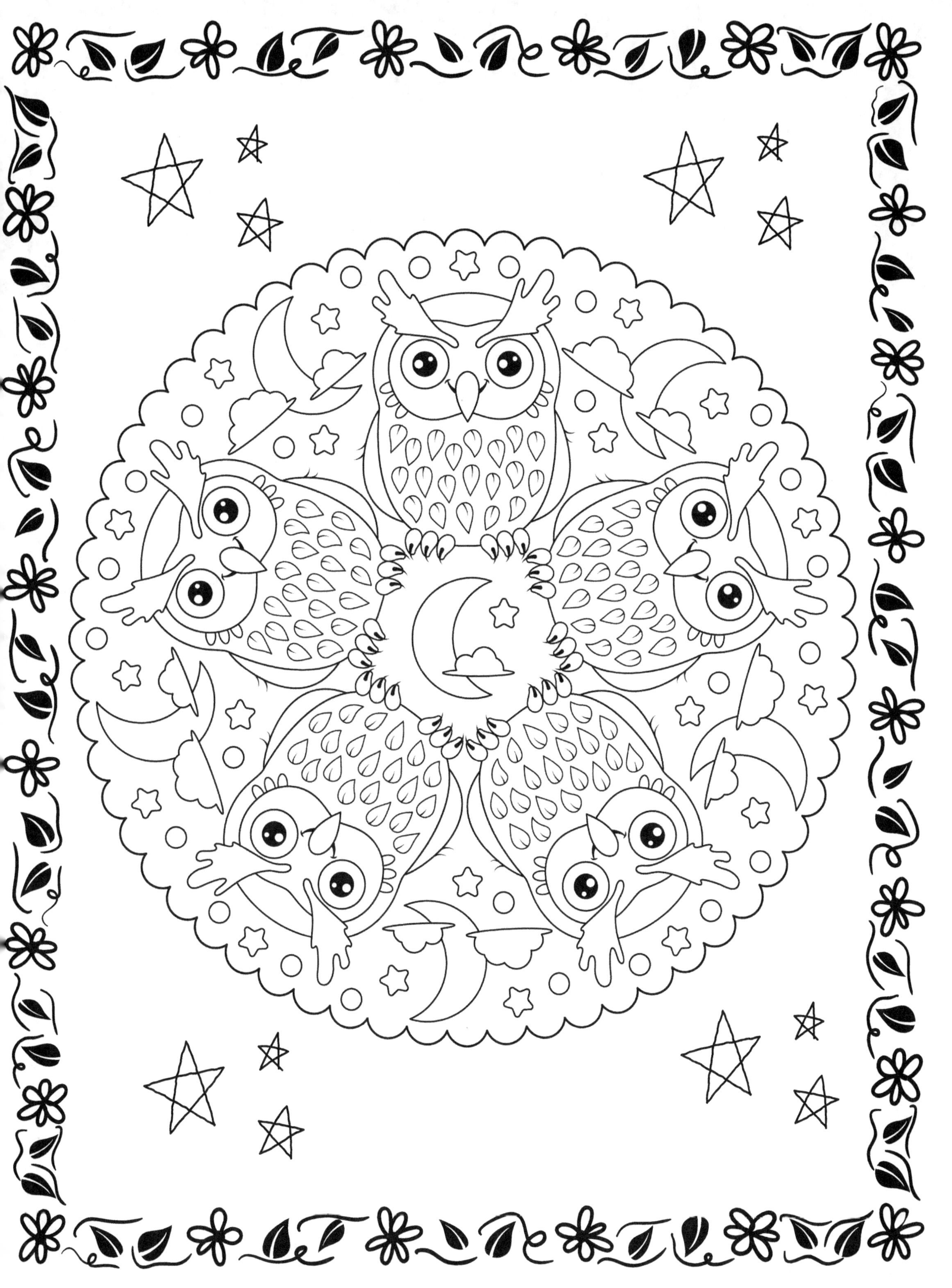

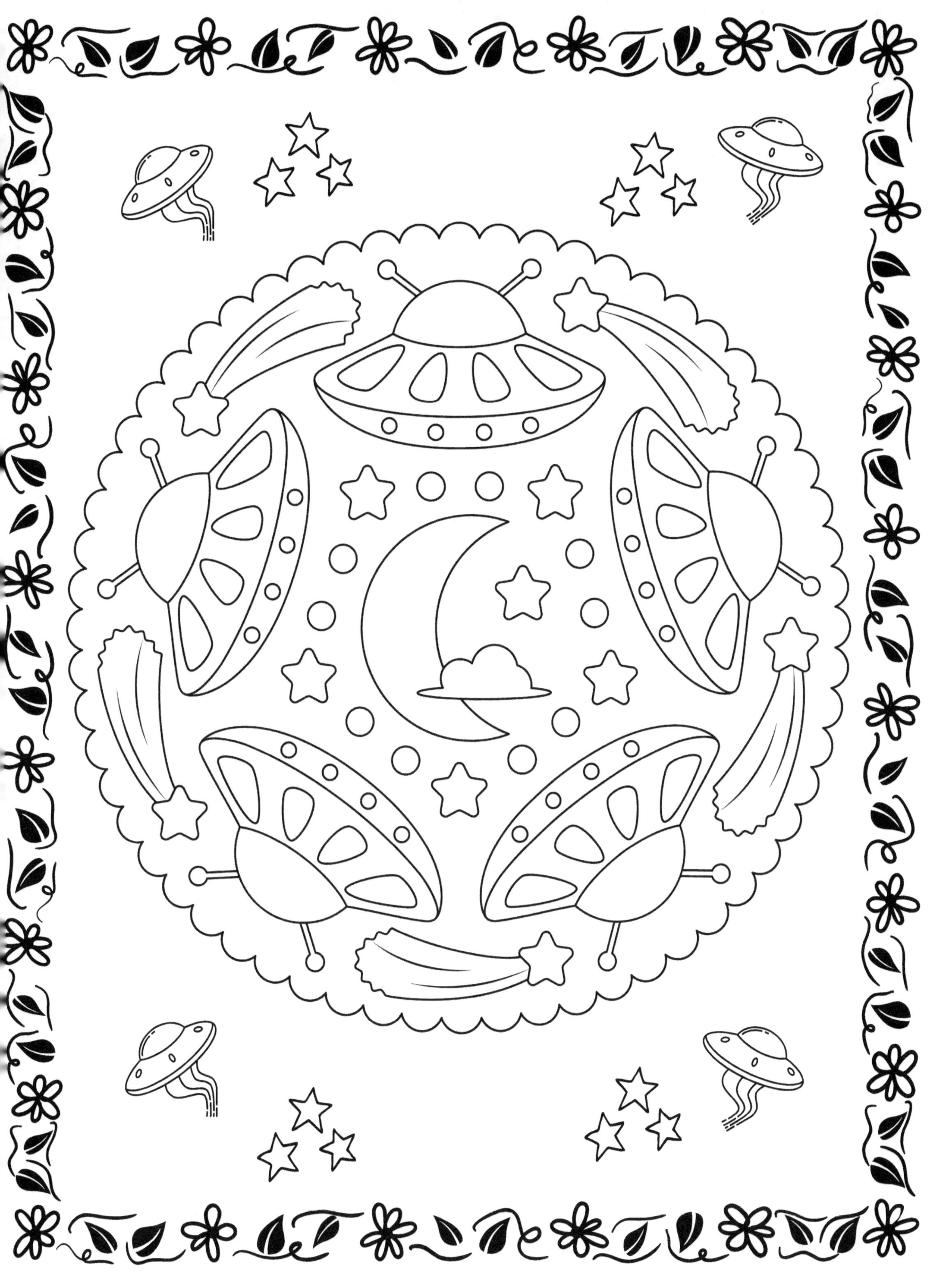

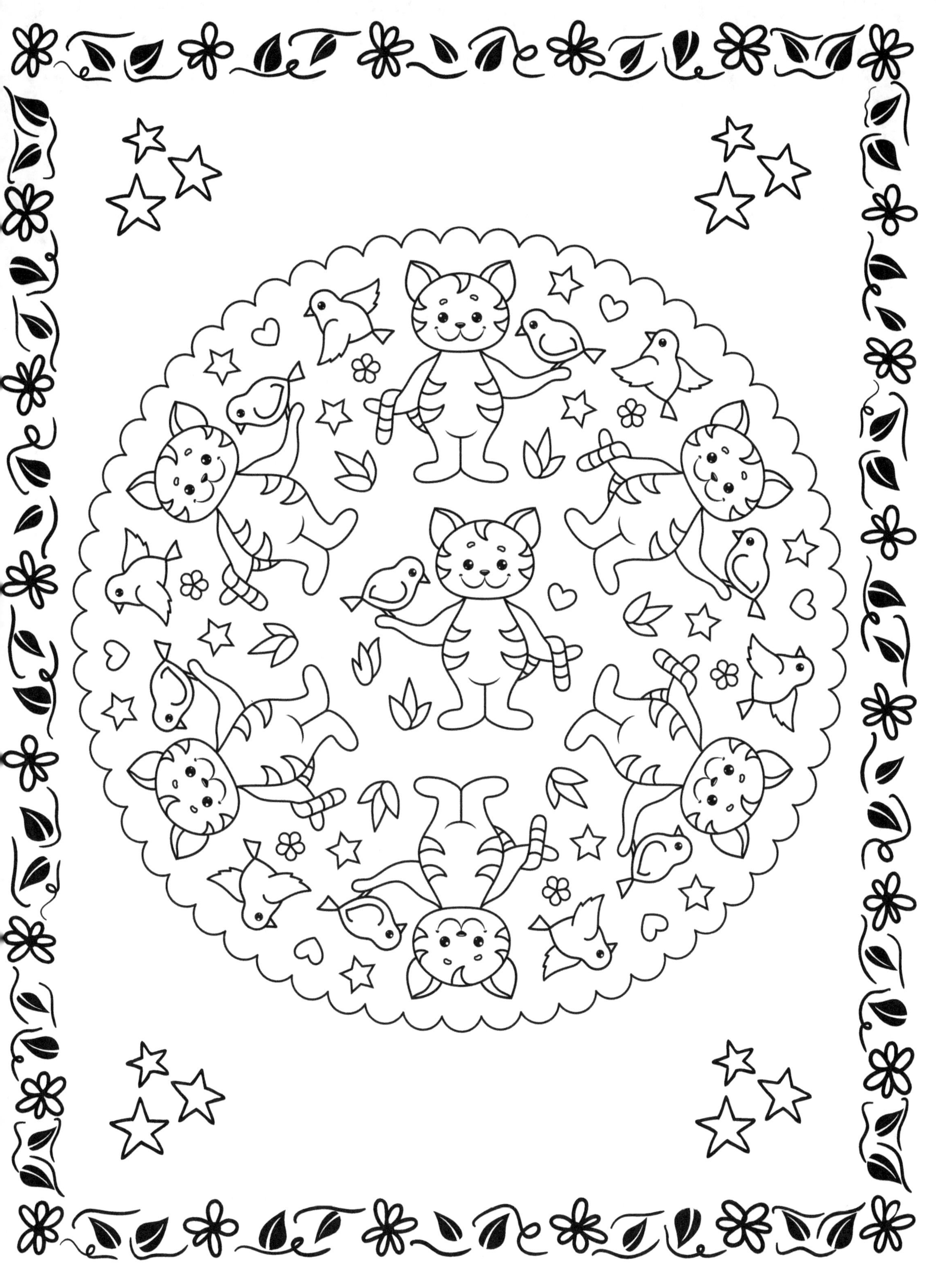

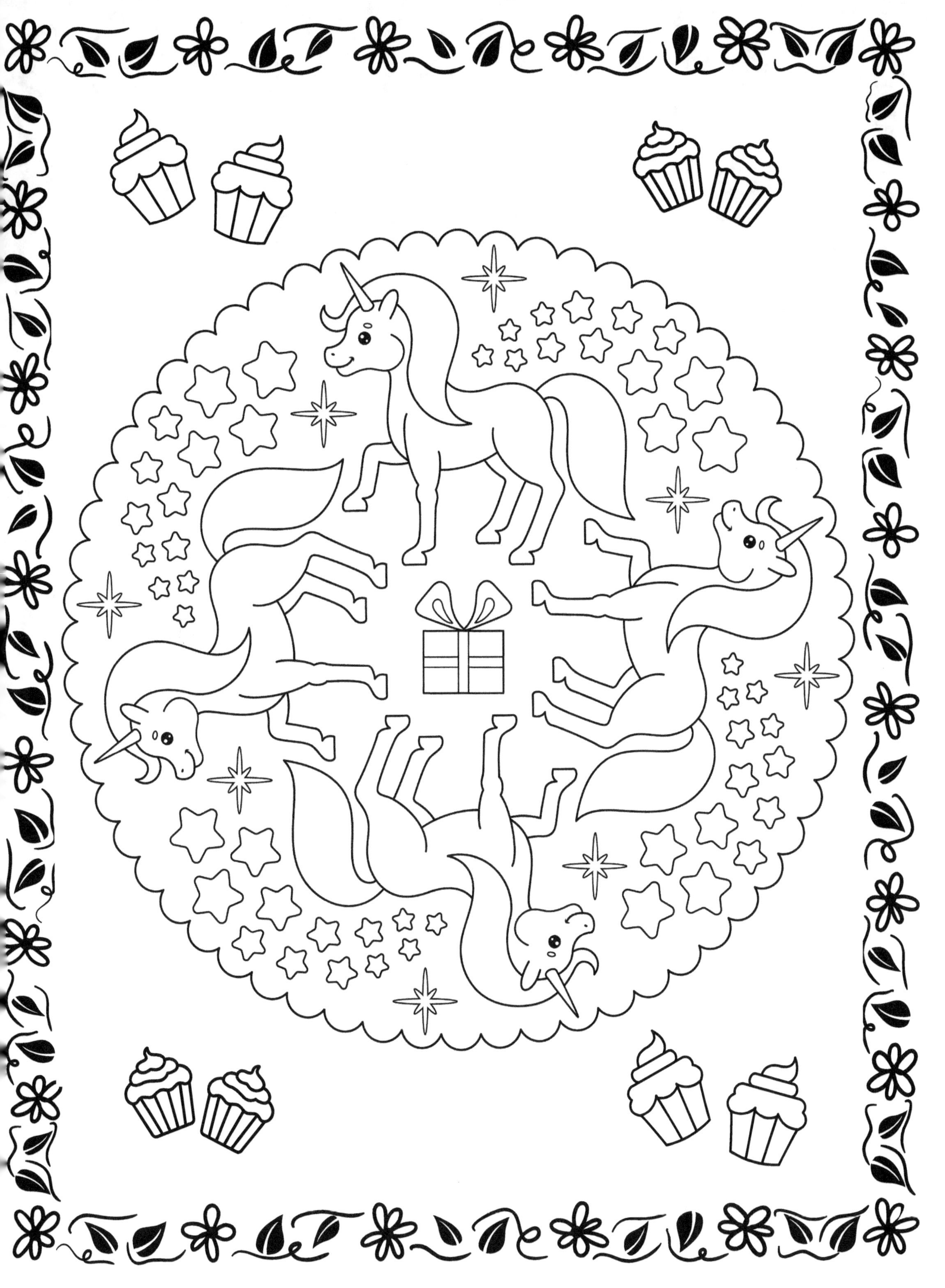

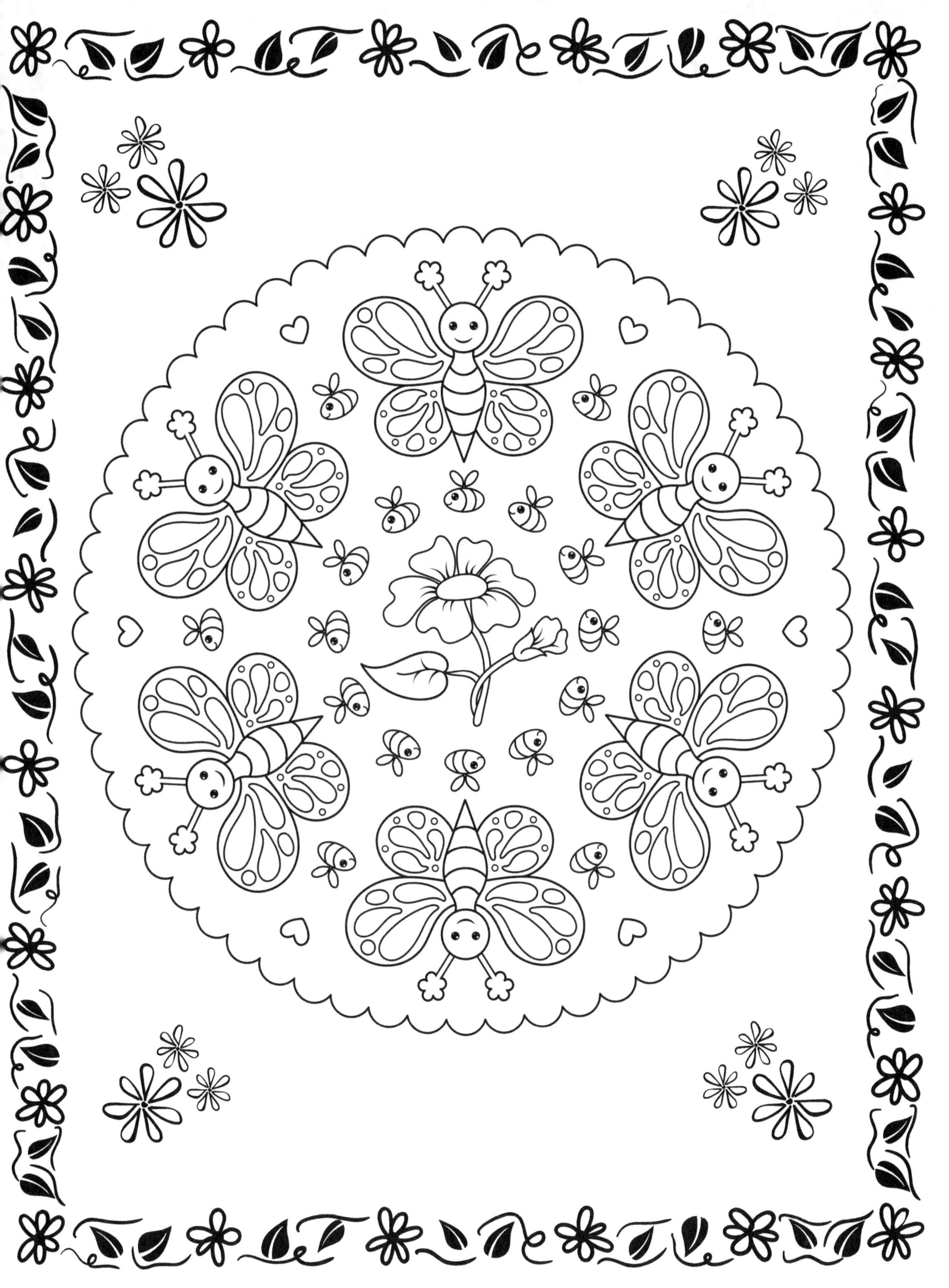

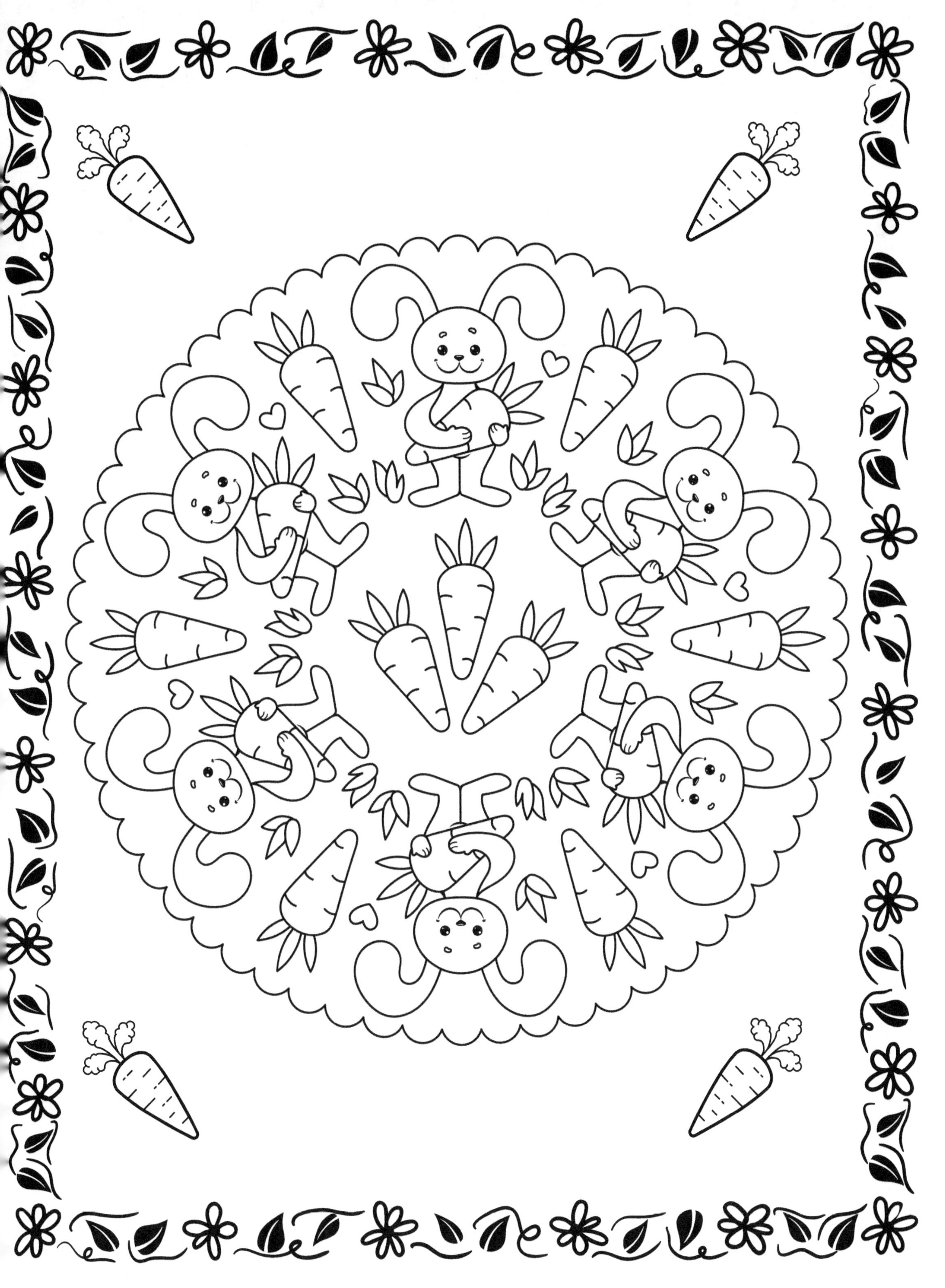

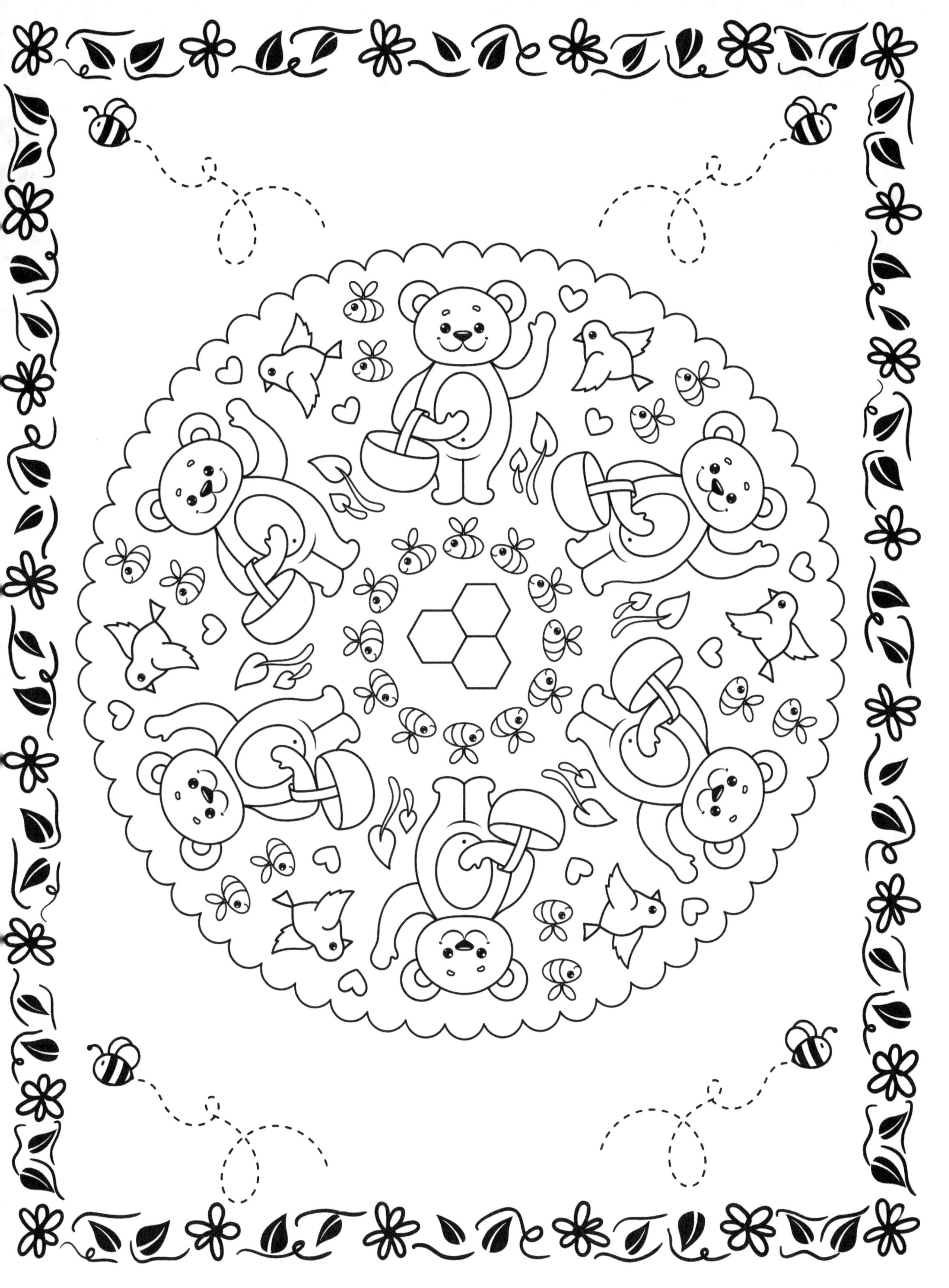

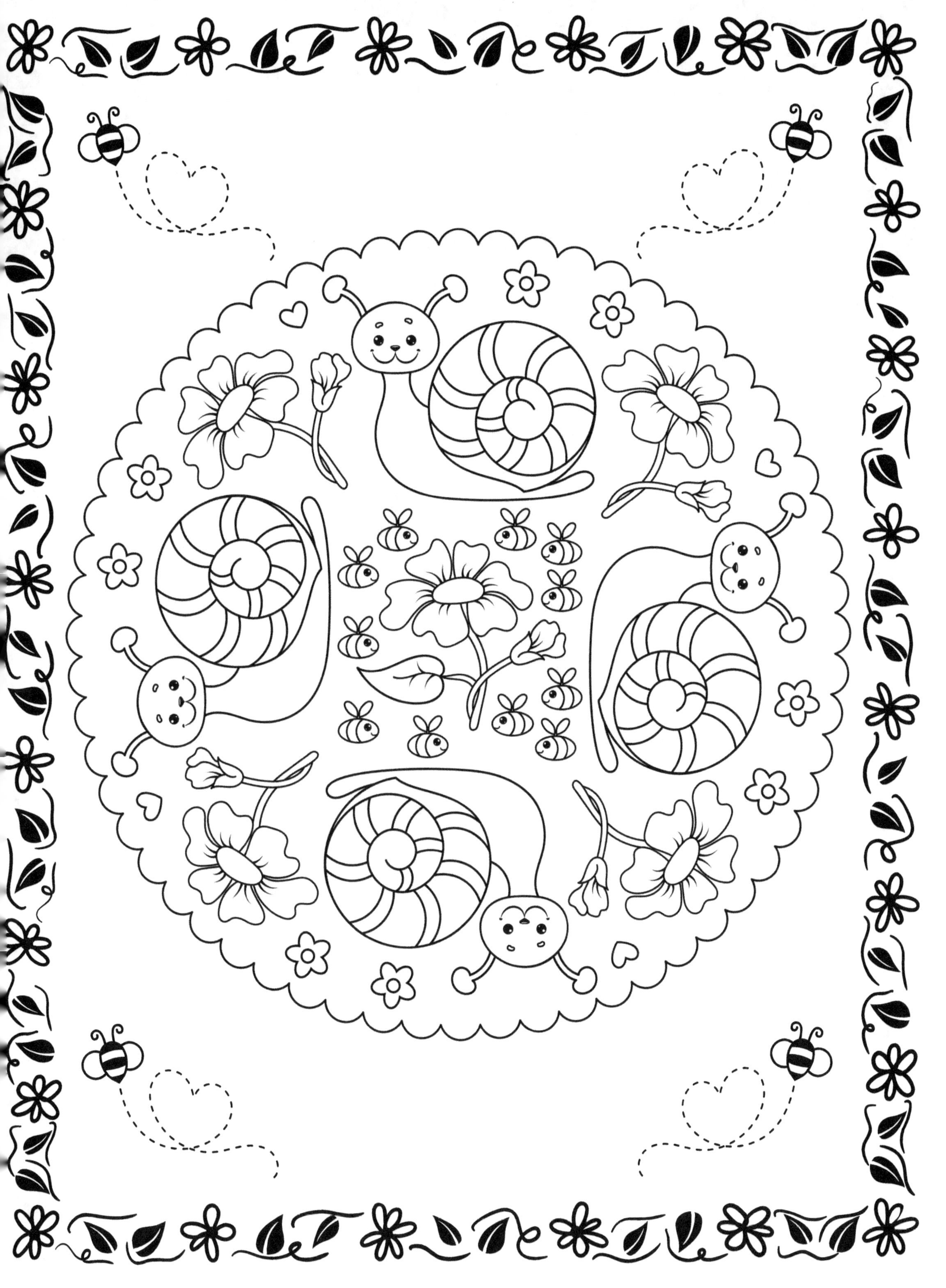

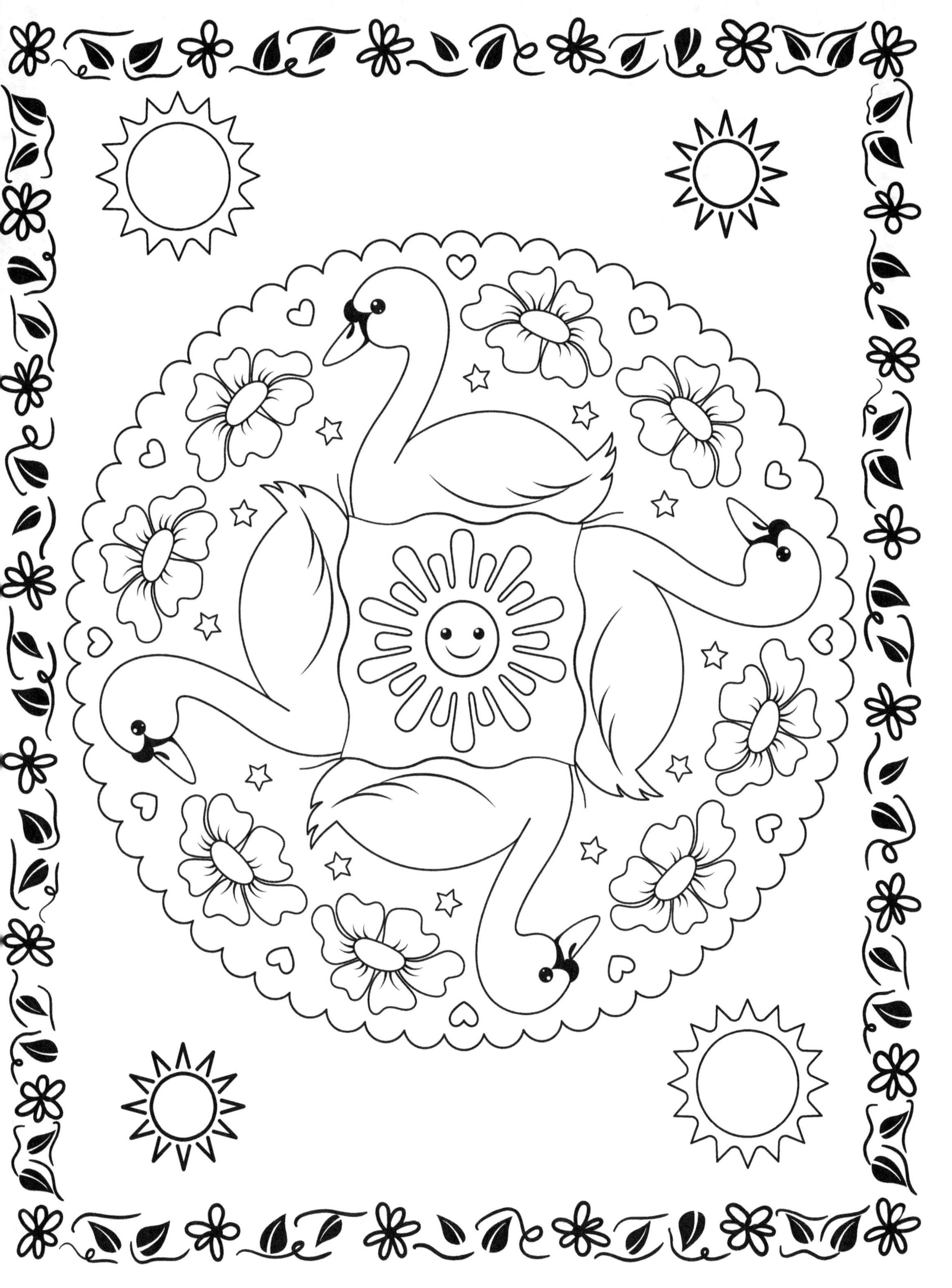

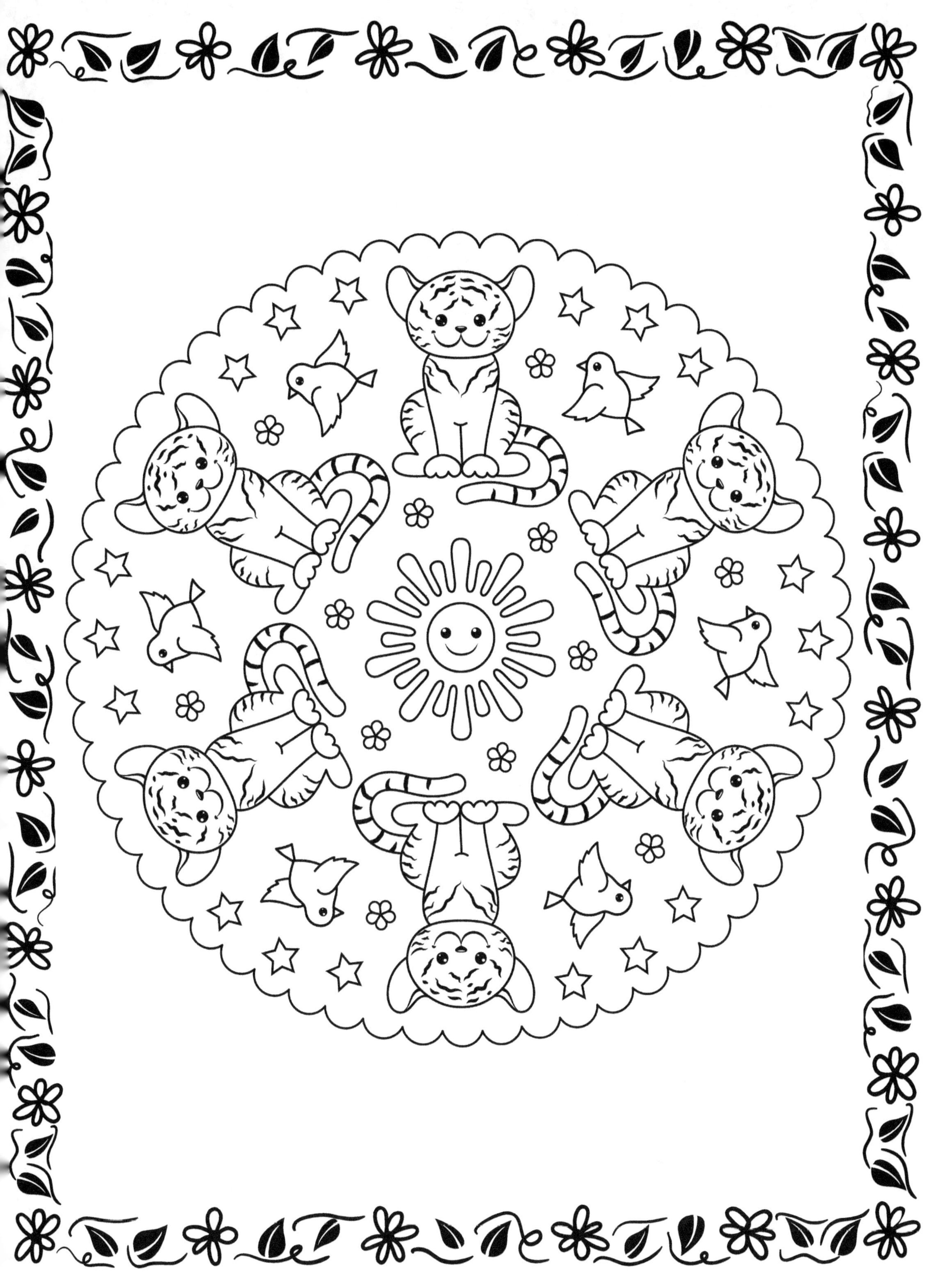

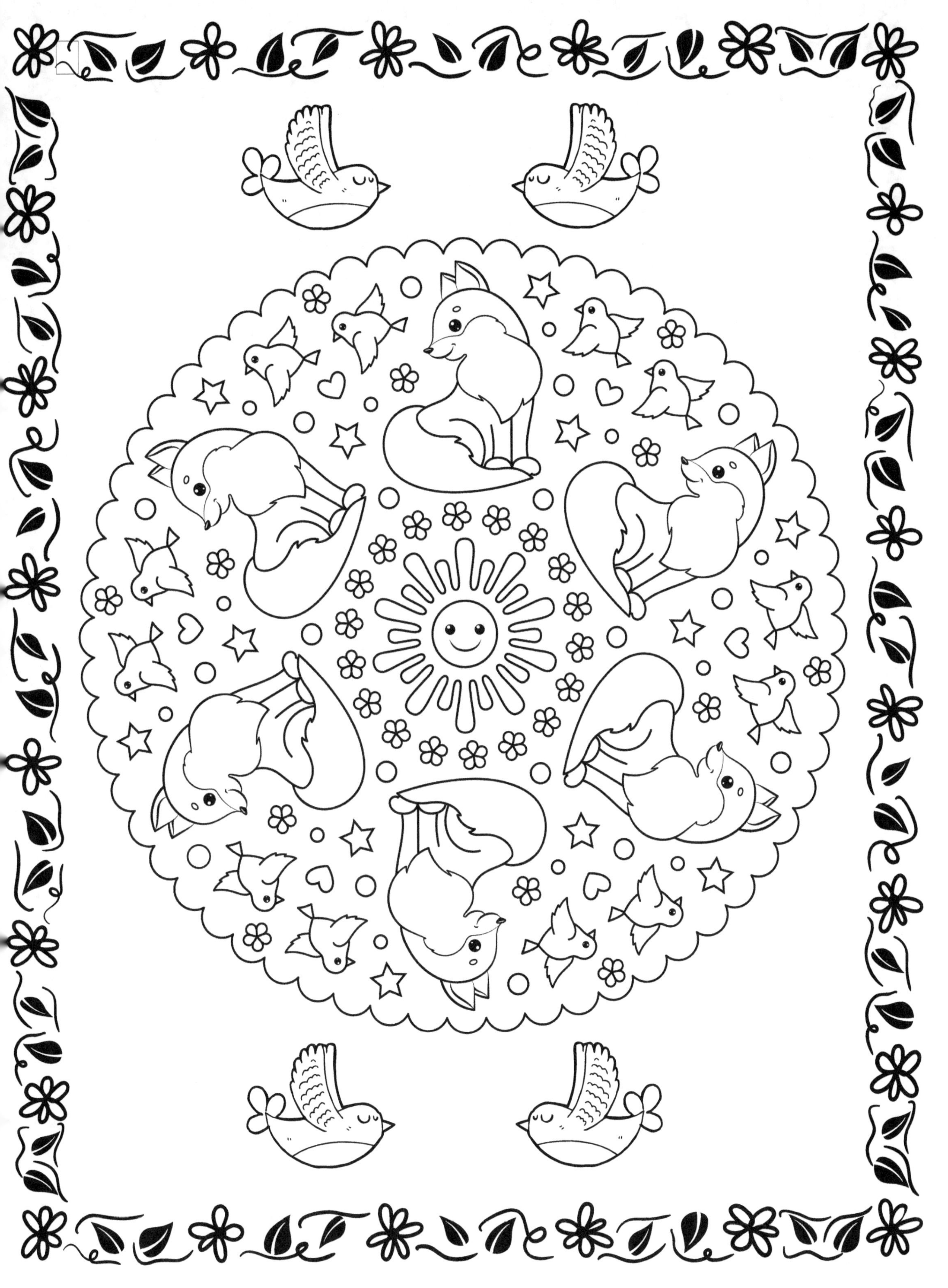

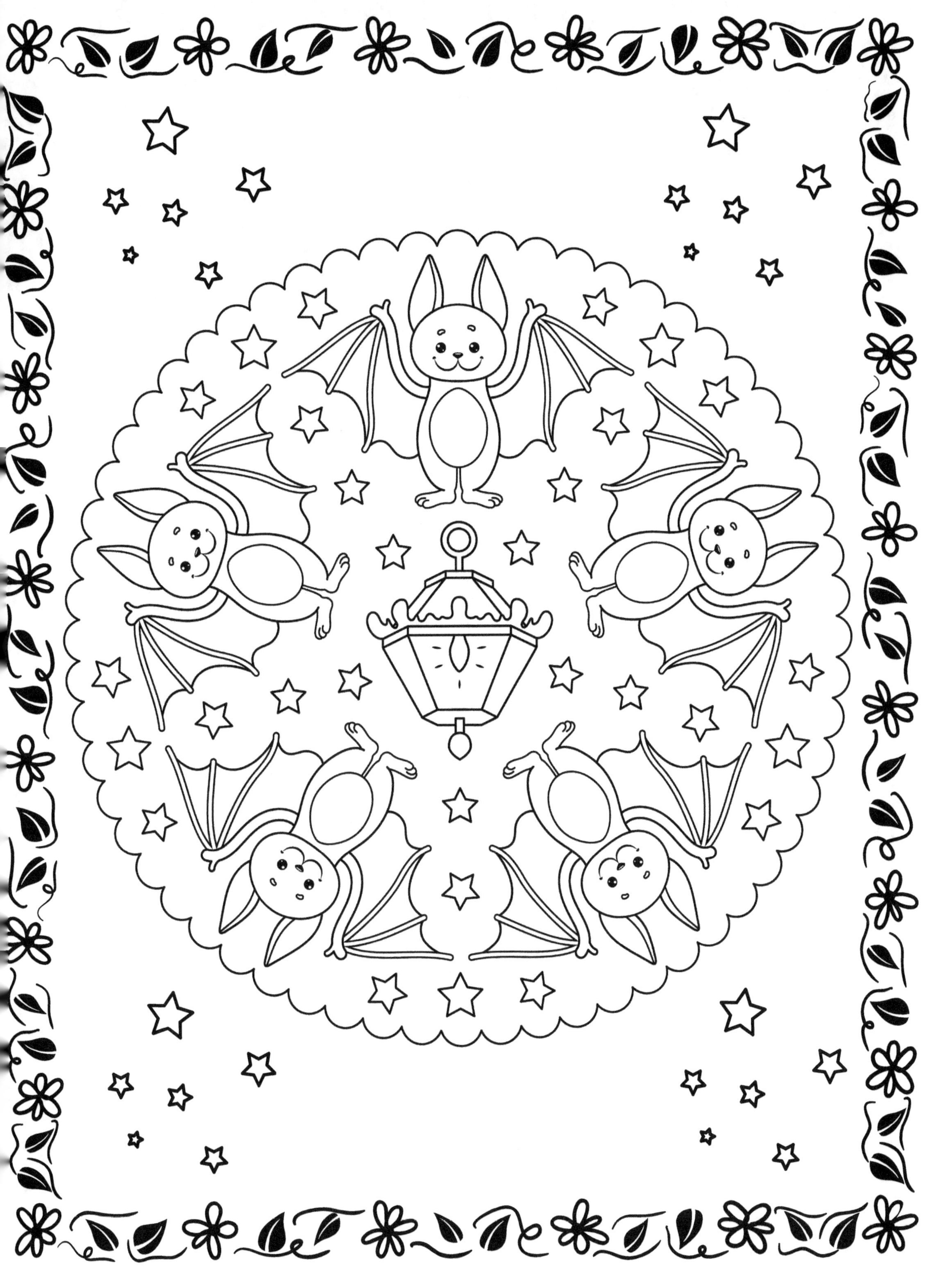

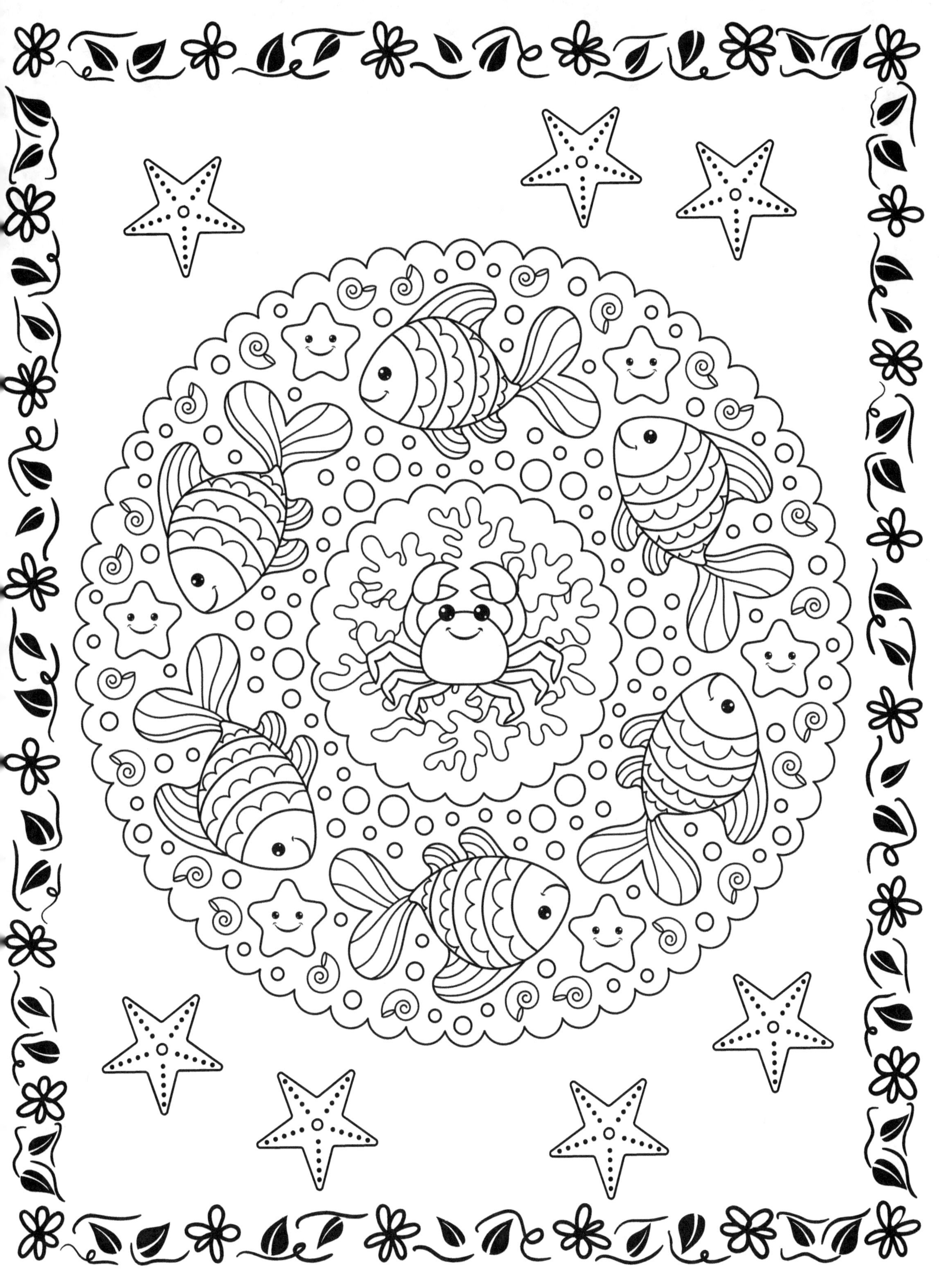

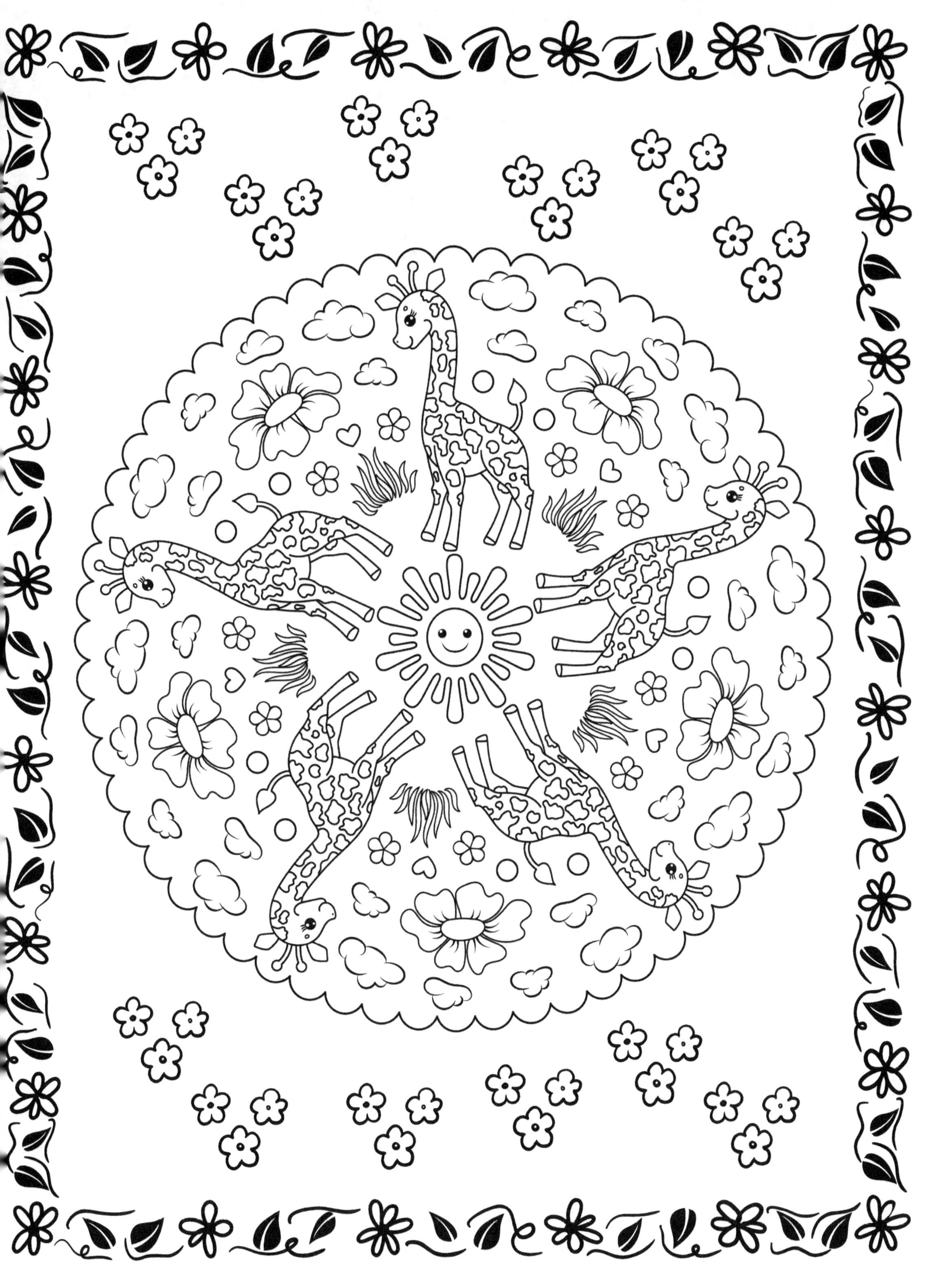

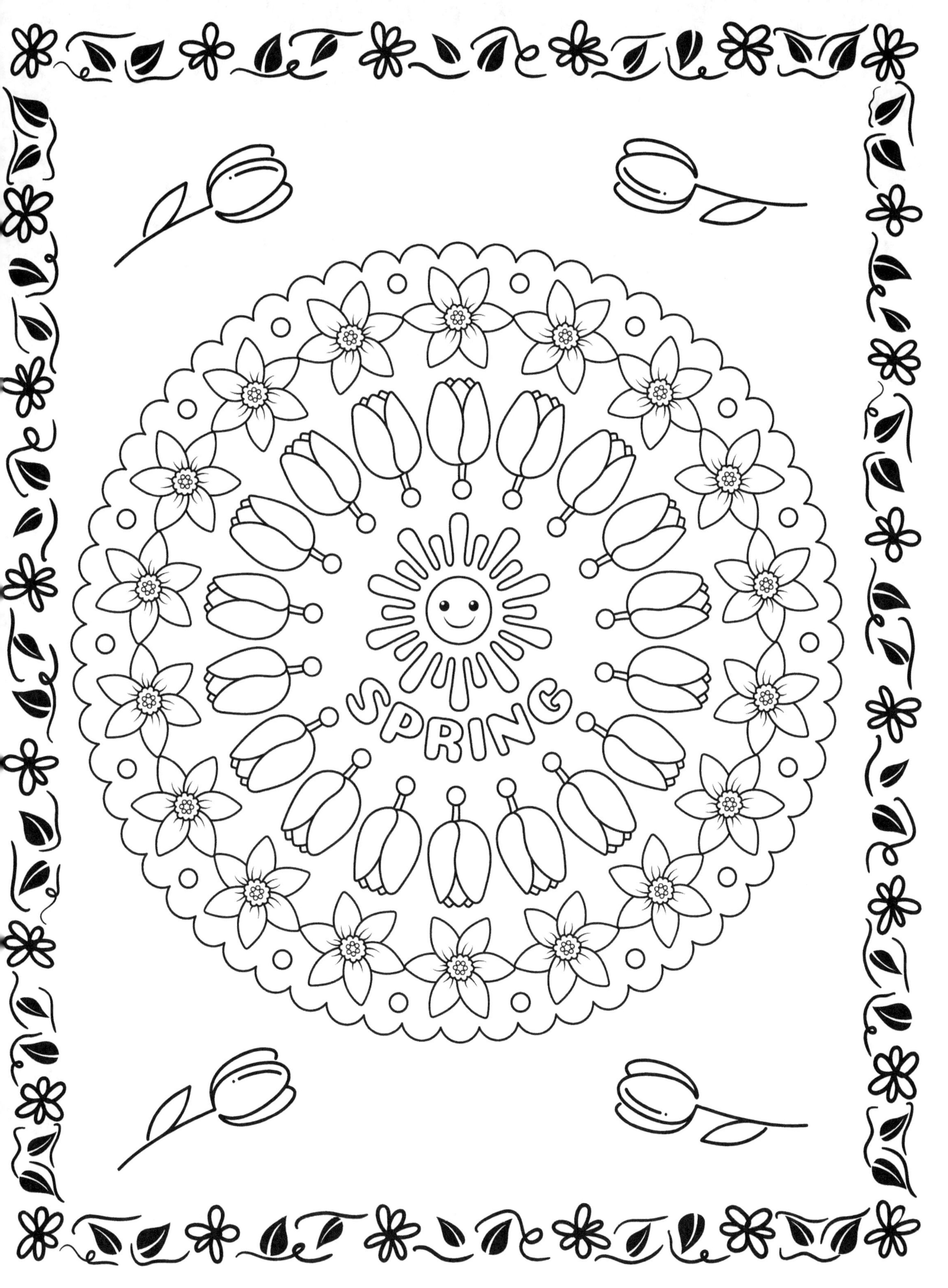
SPRING

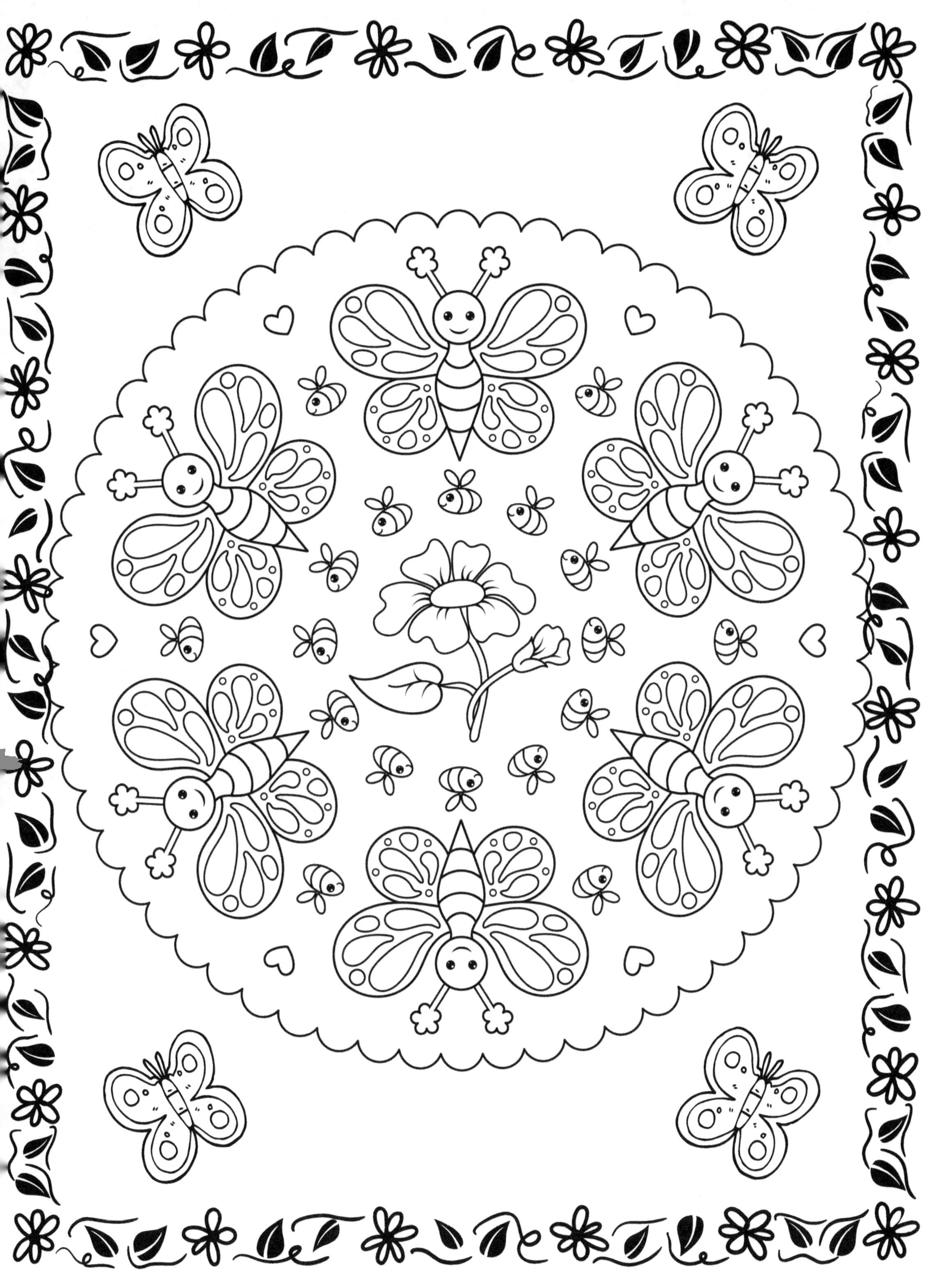

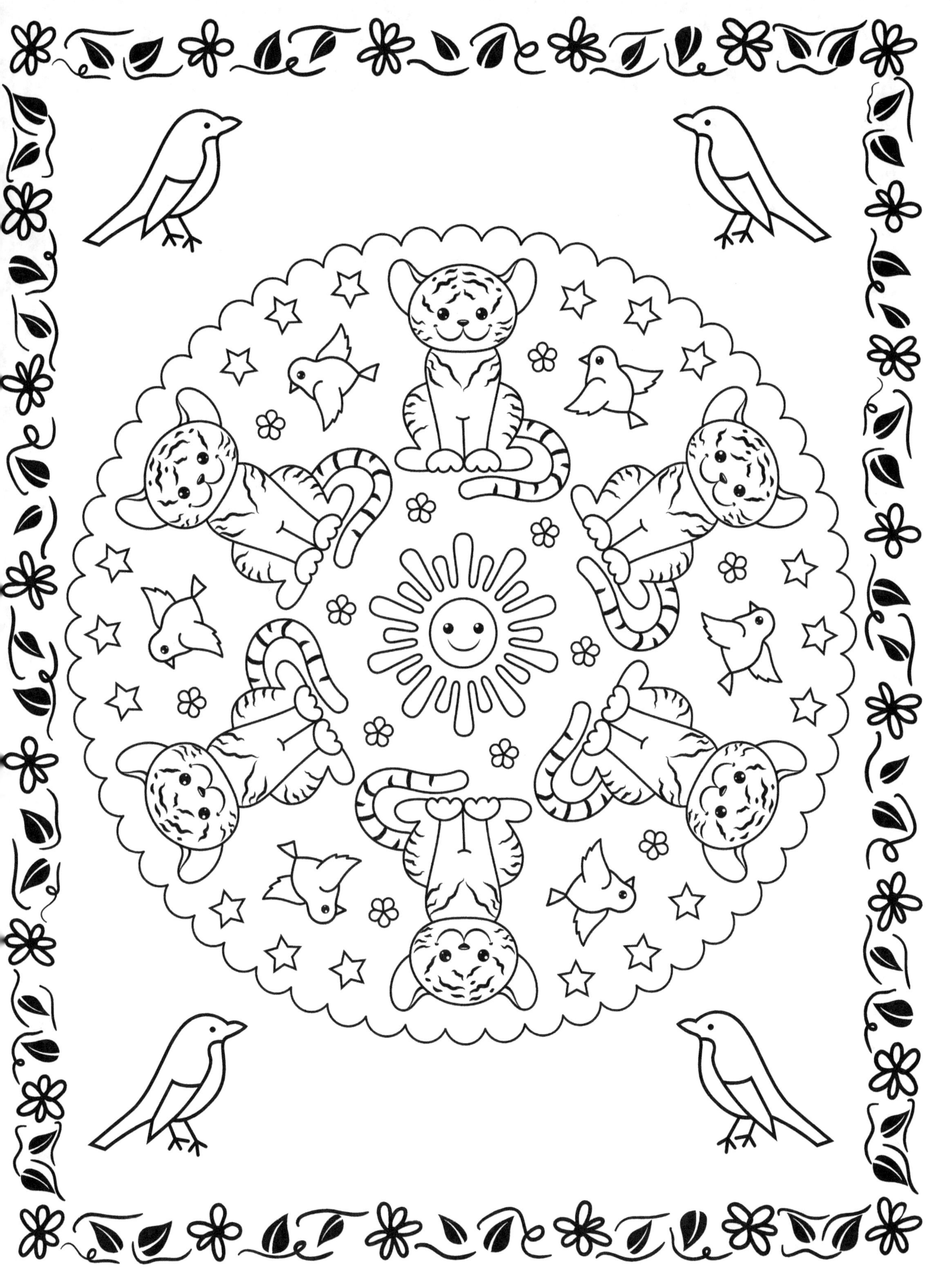

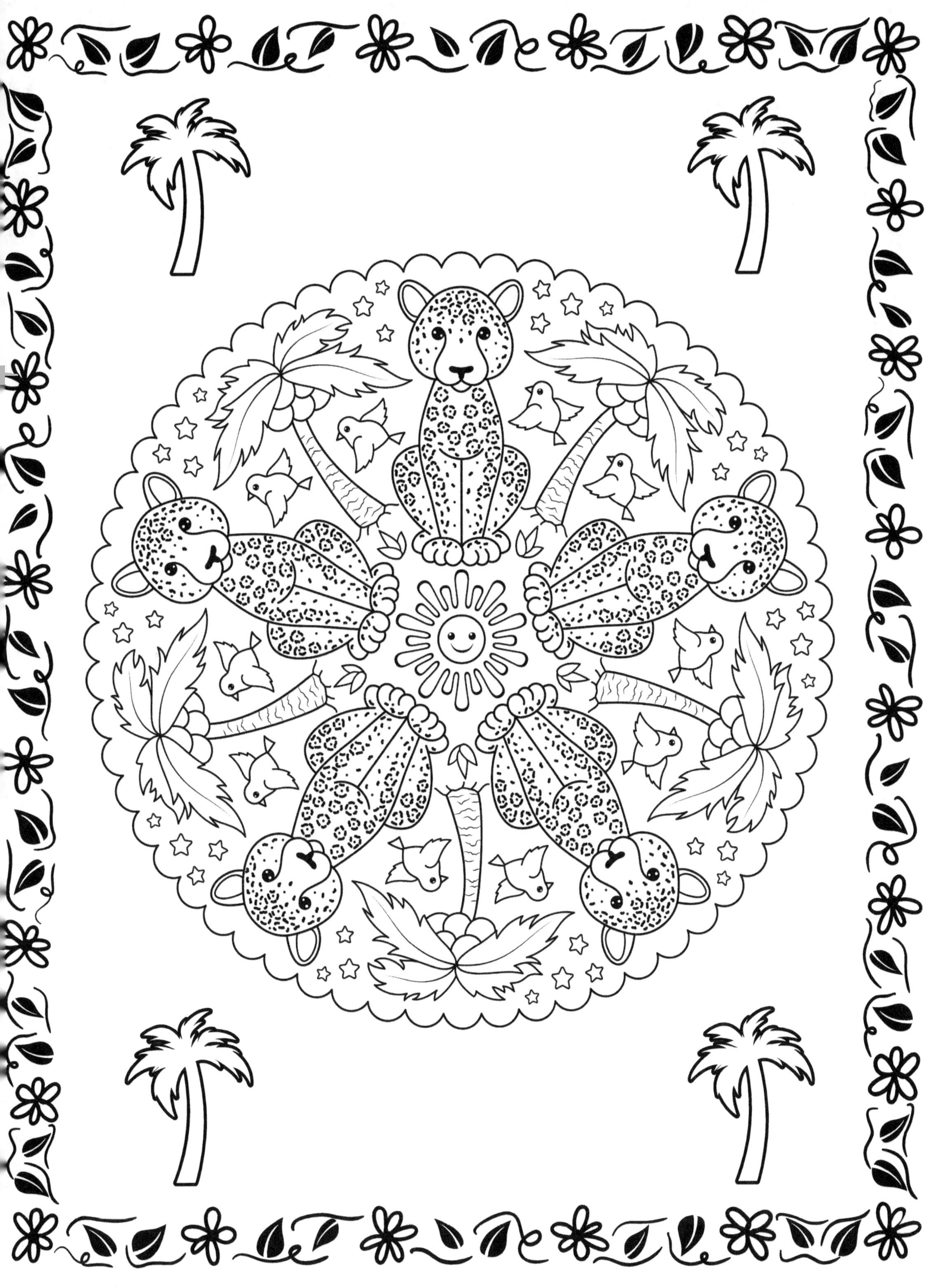

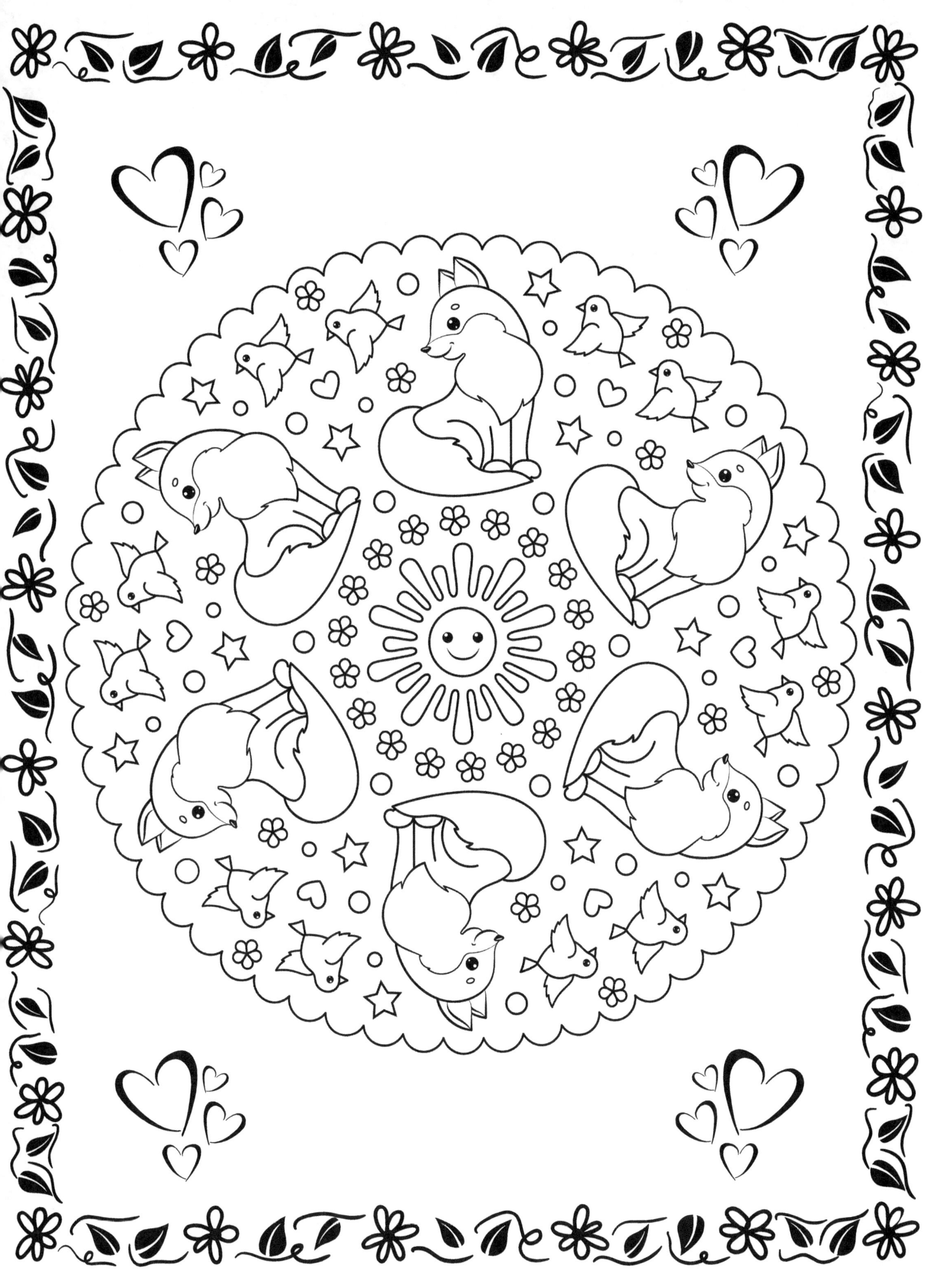

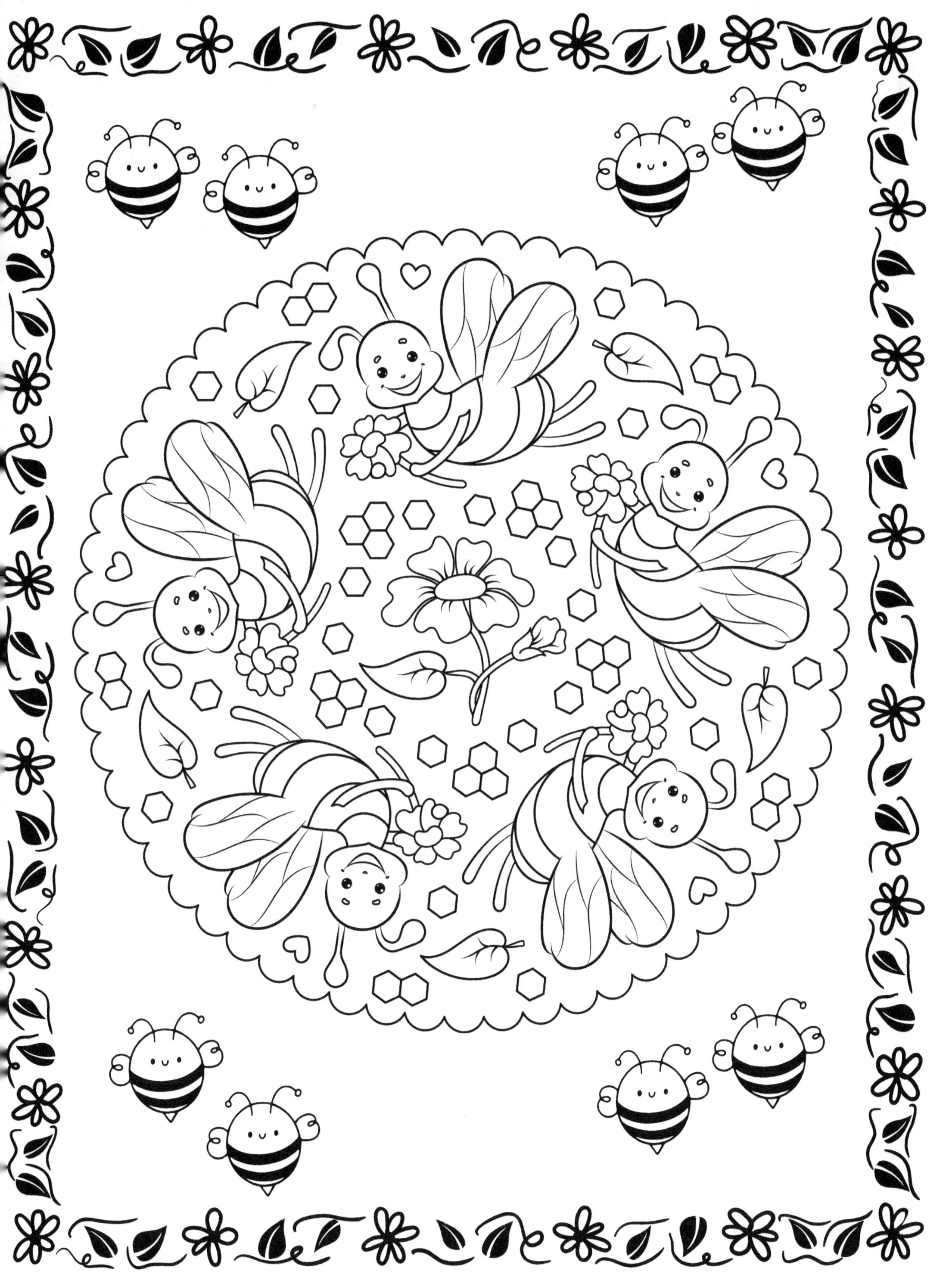

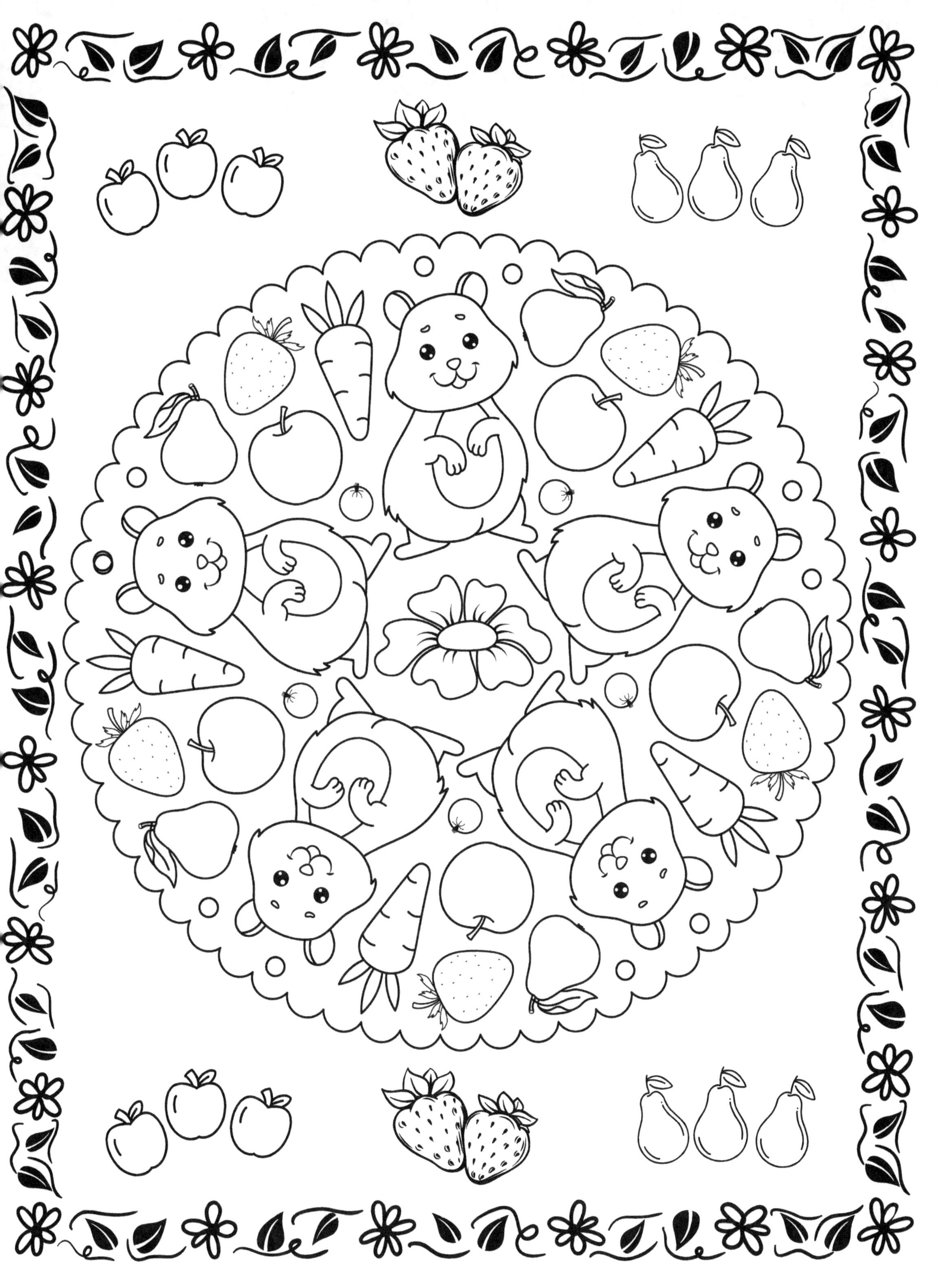

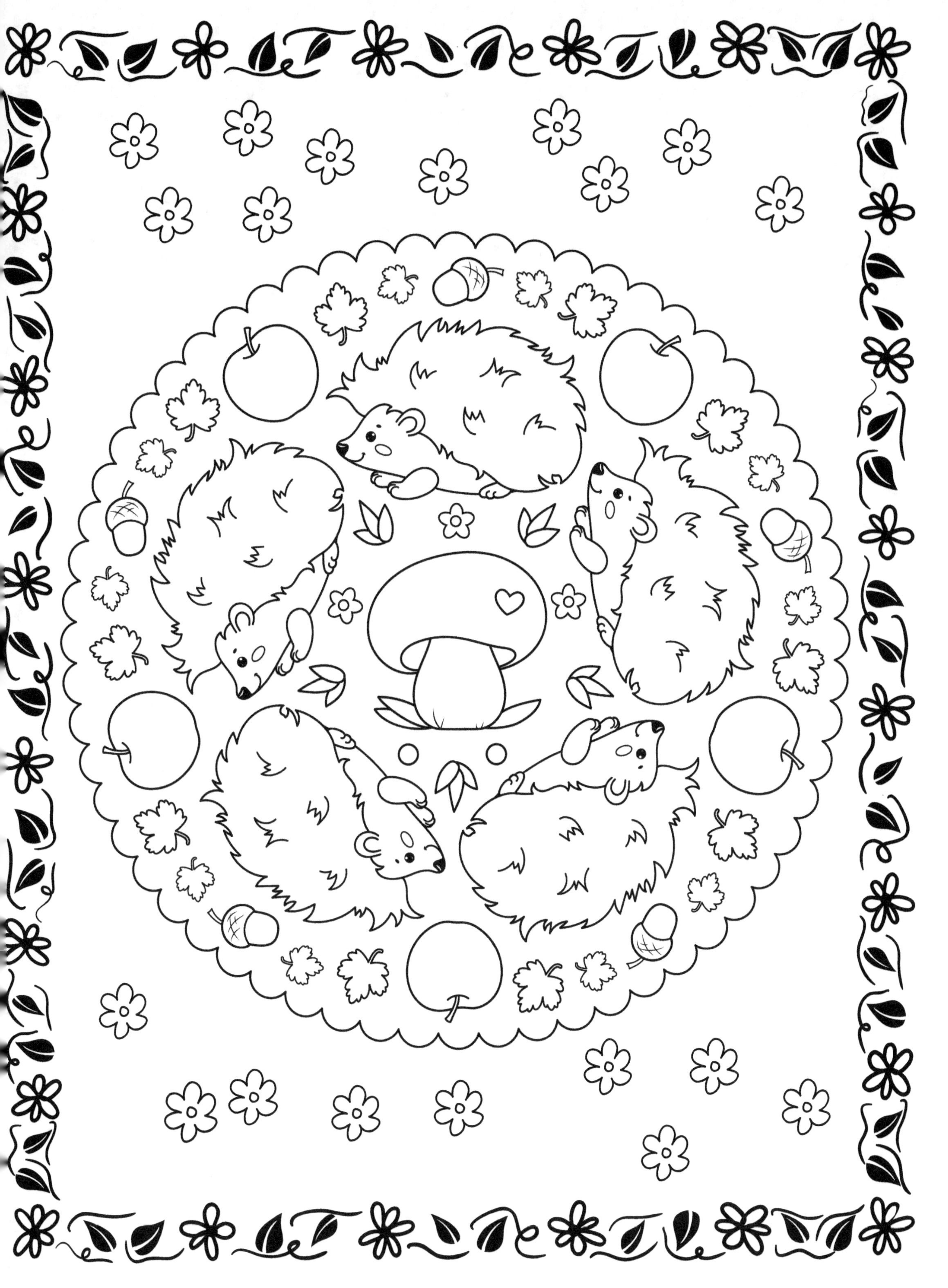

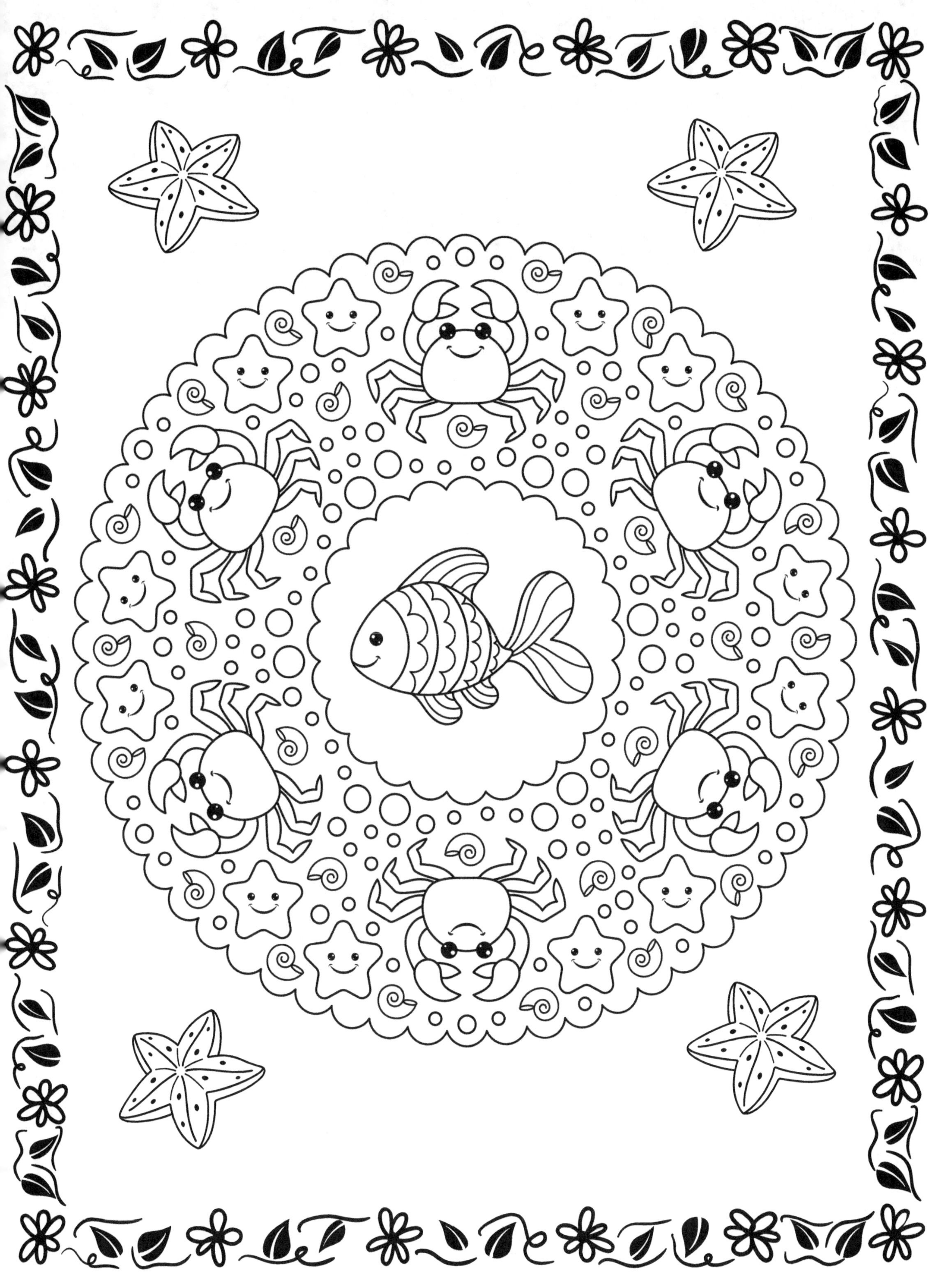

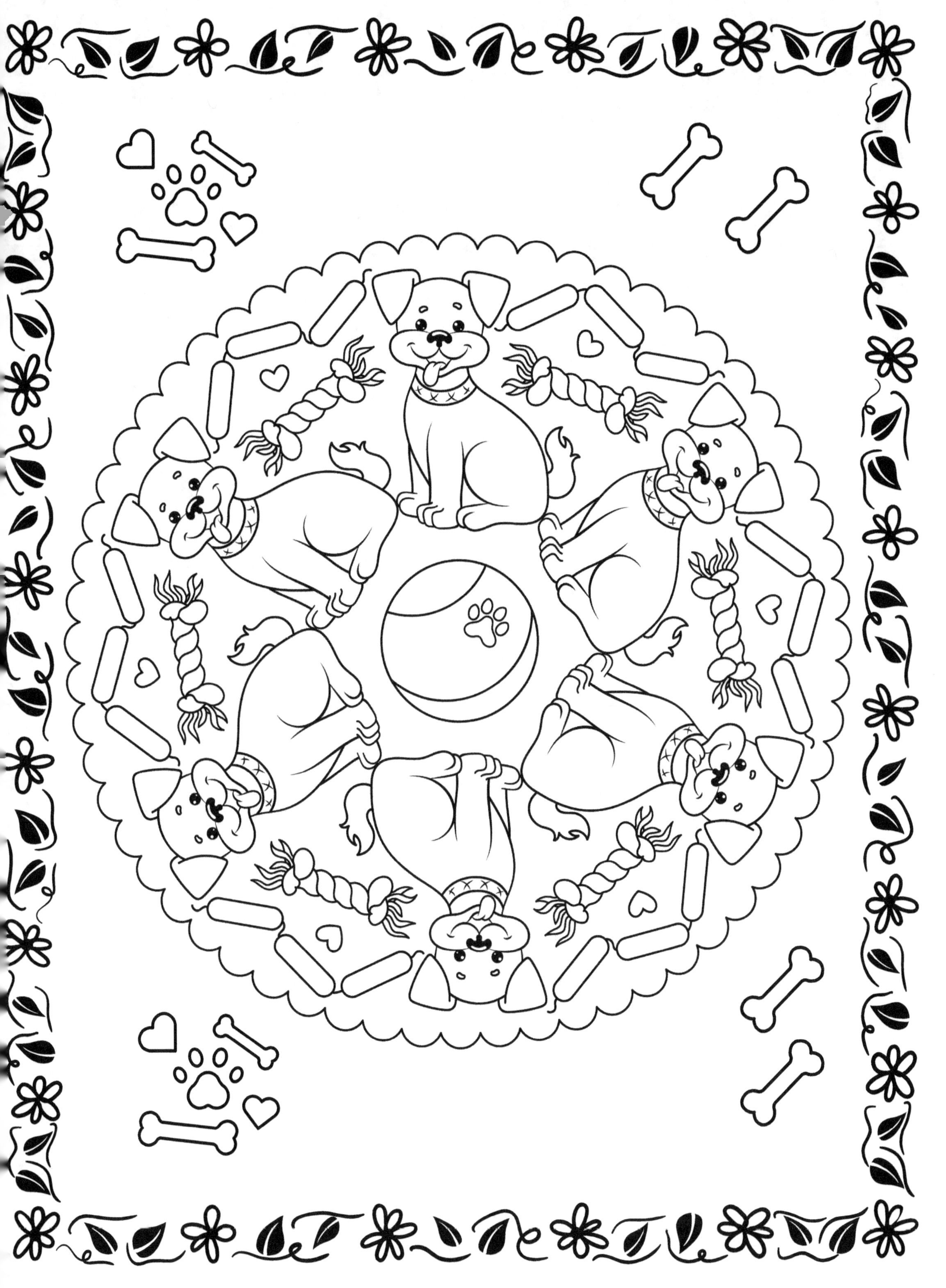

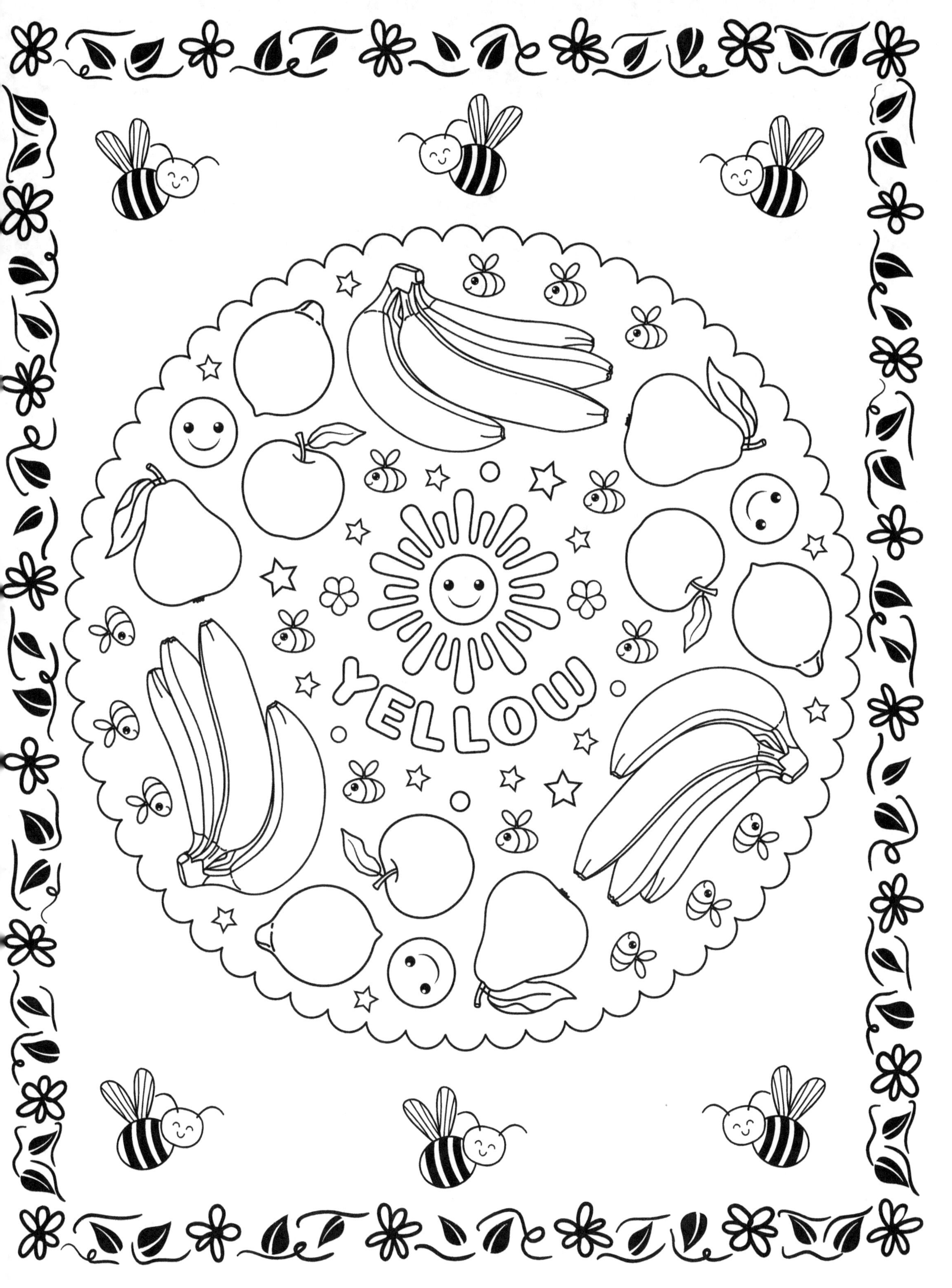
YELLOW

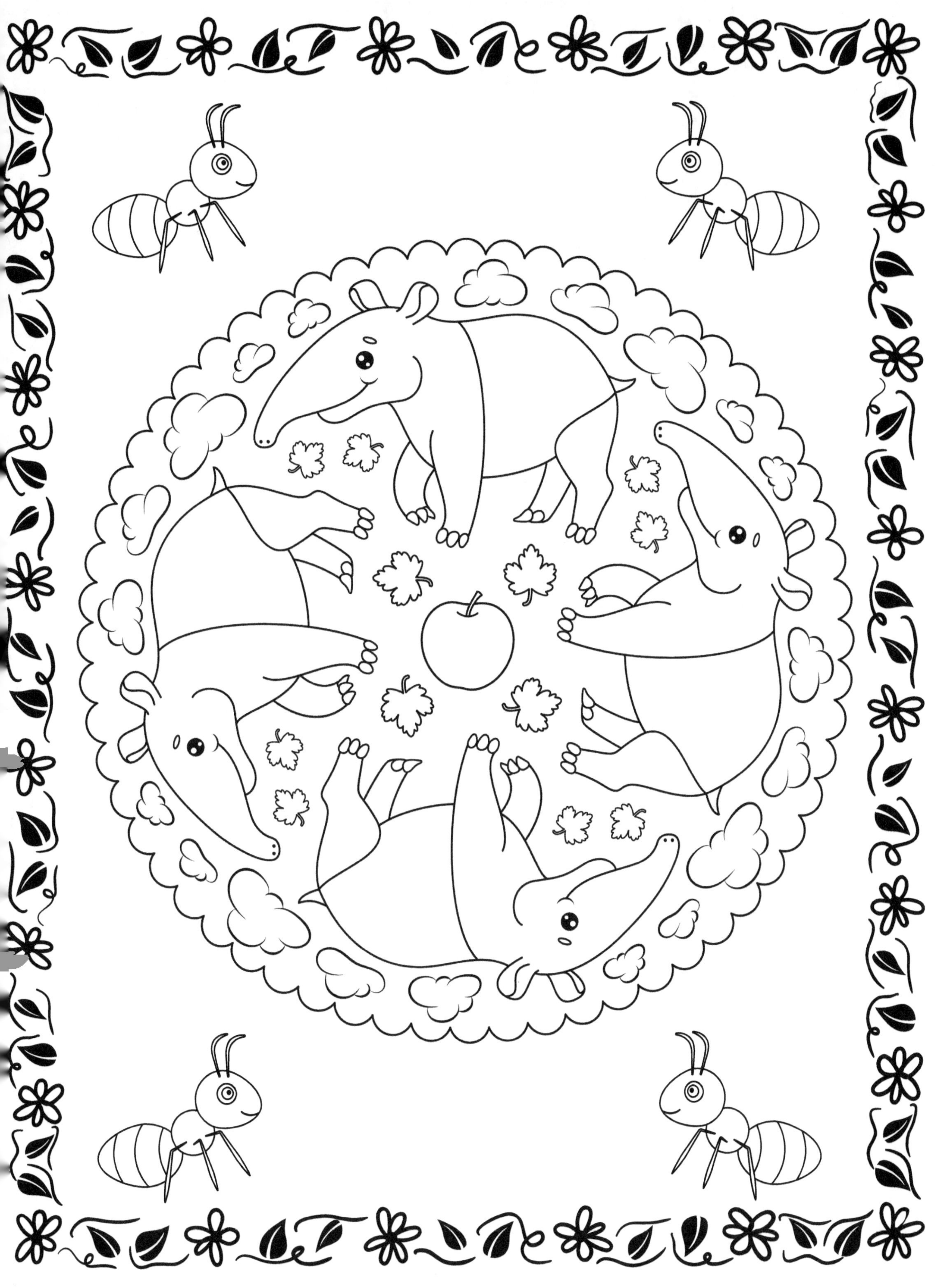

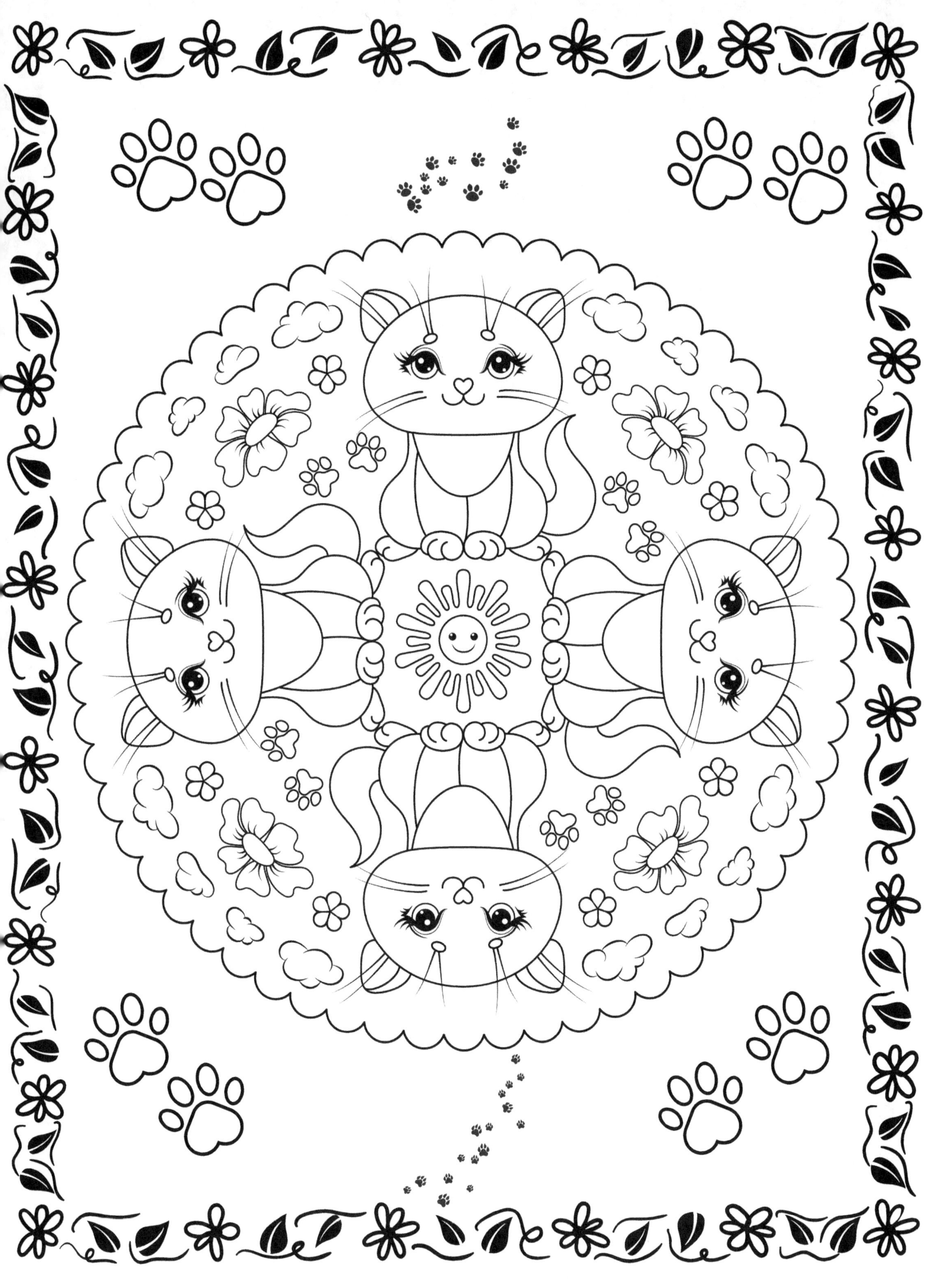

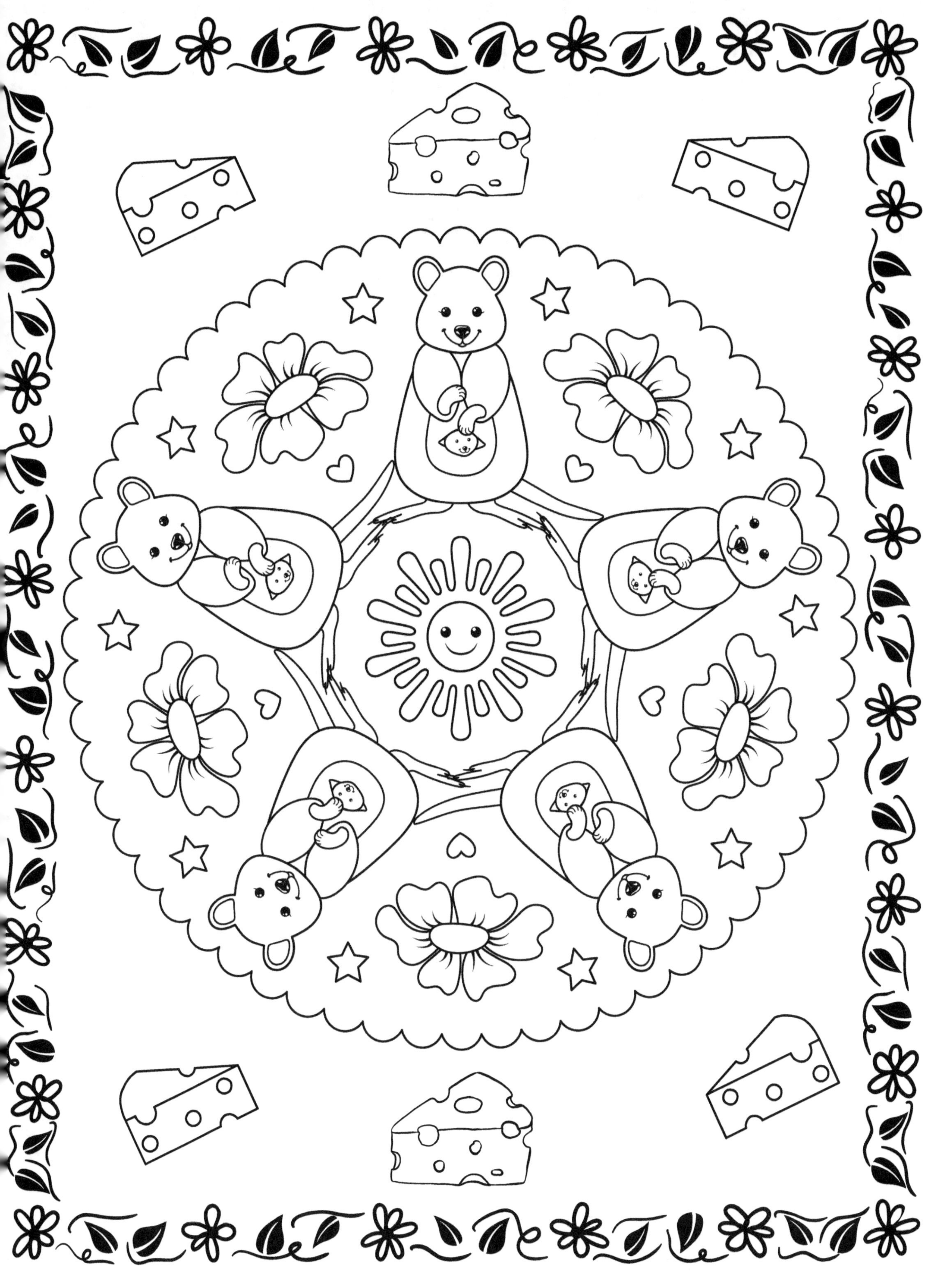

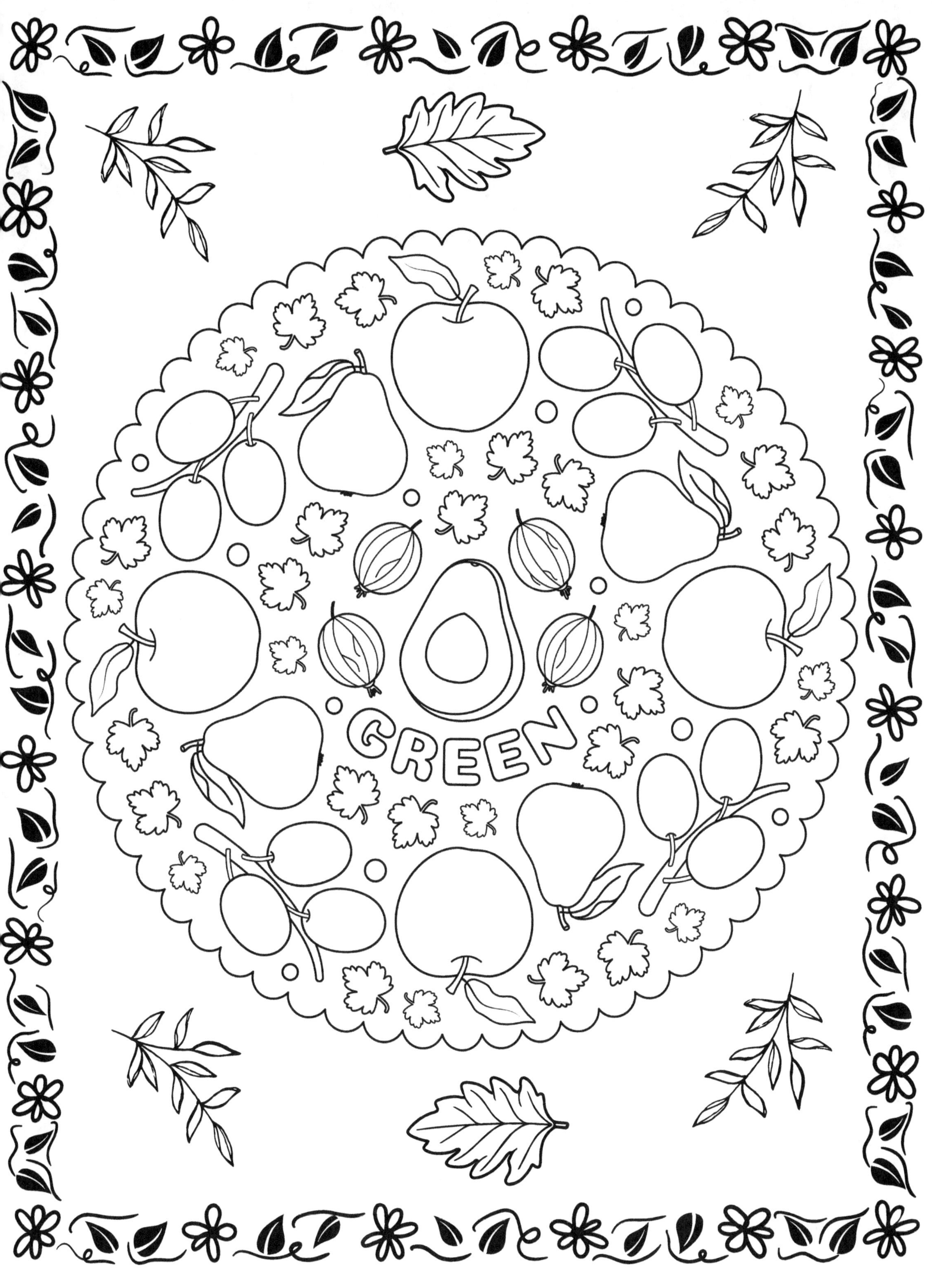
GREEN

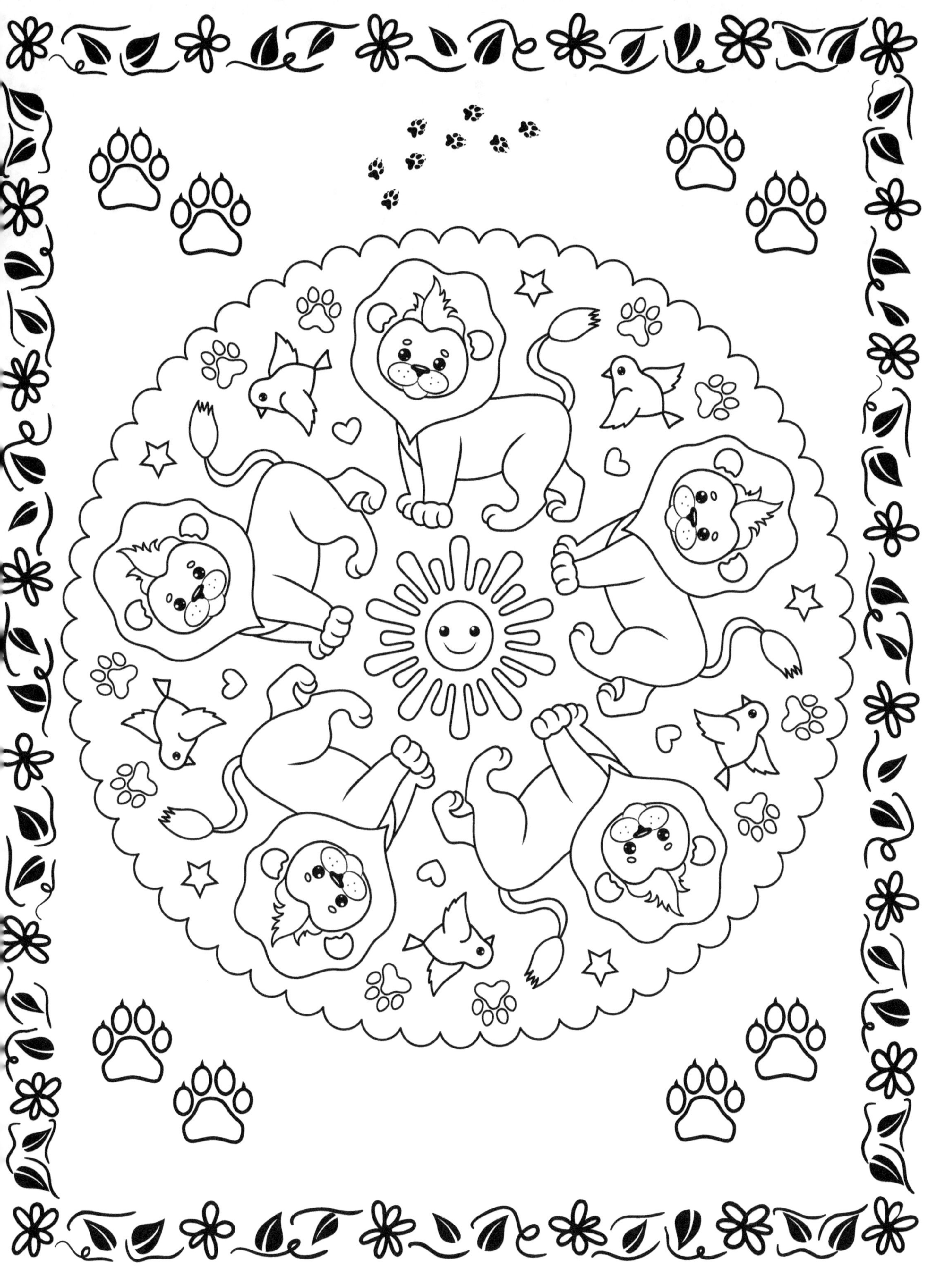

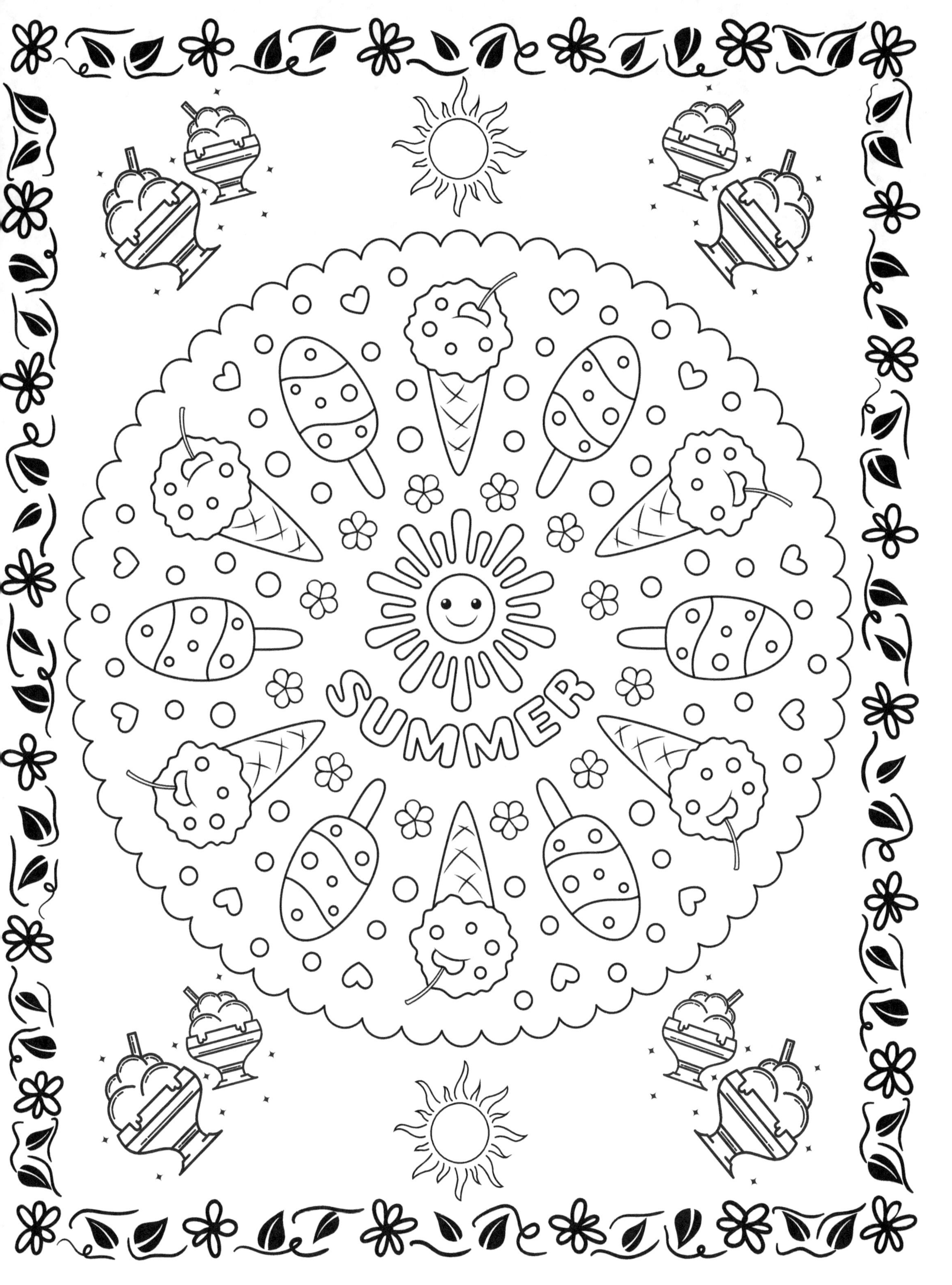

SUMMER

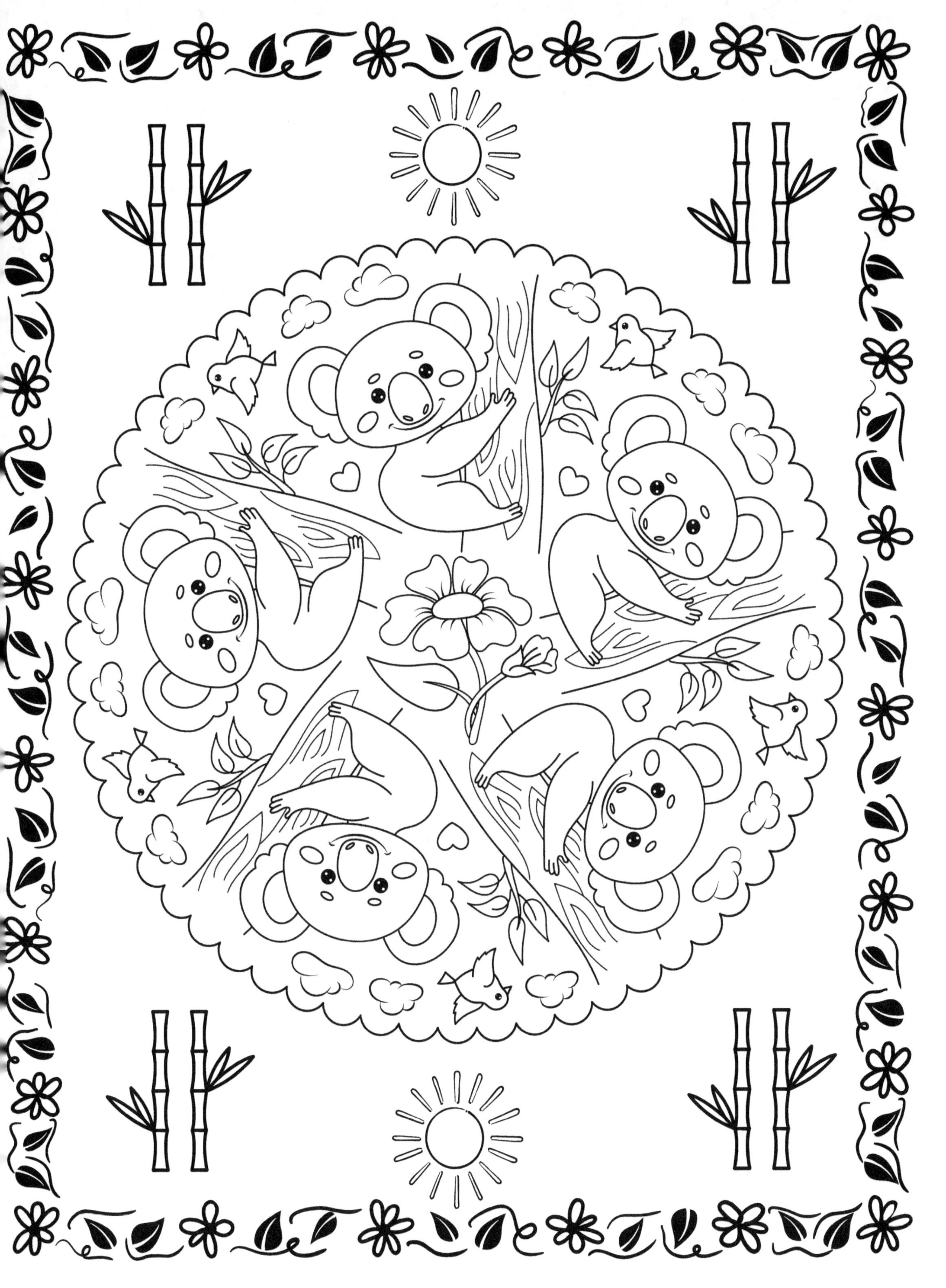

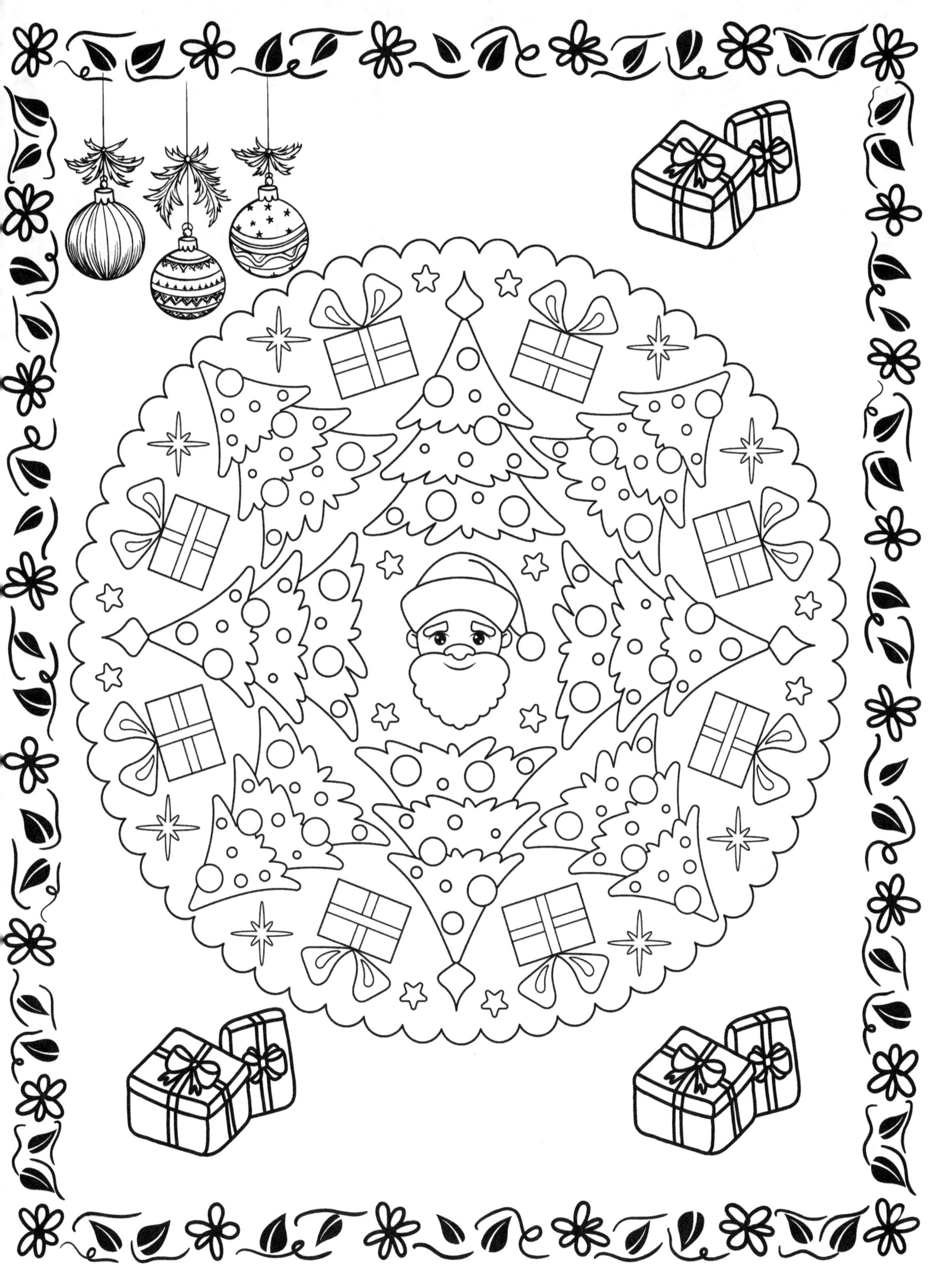

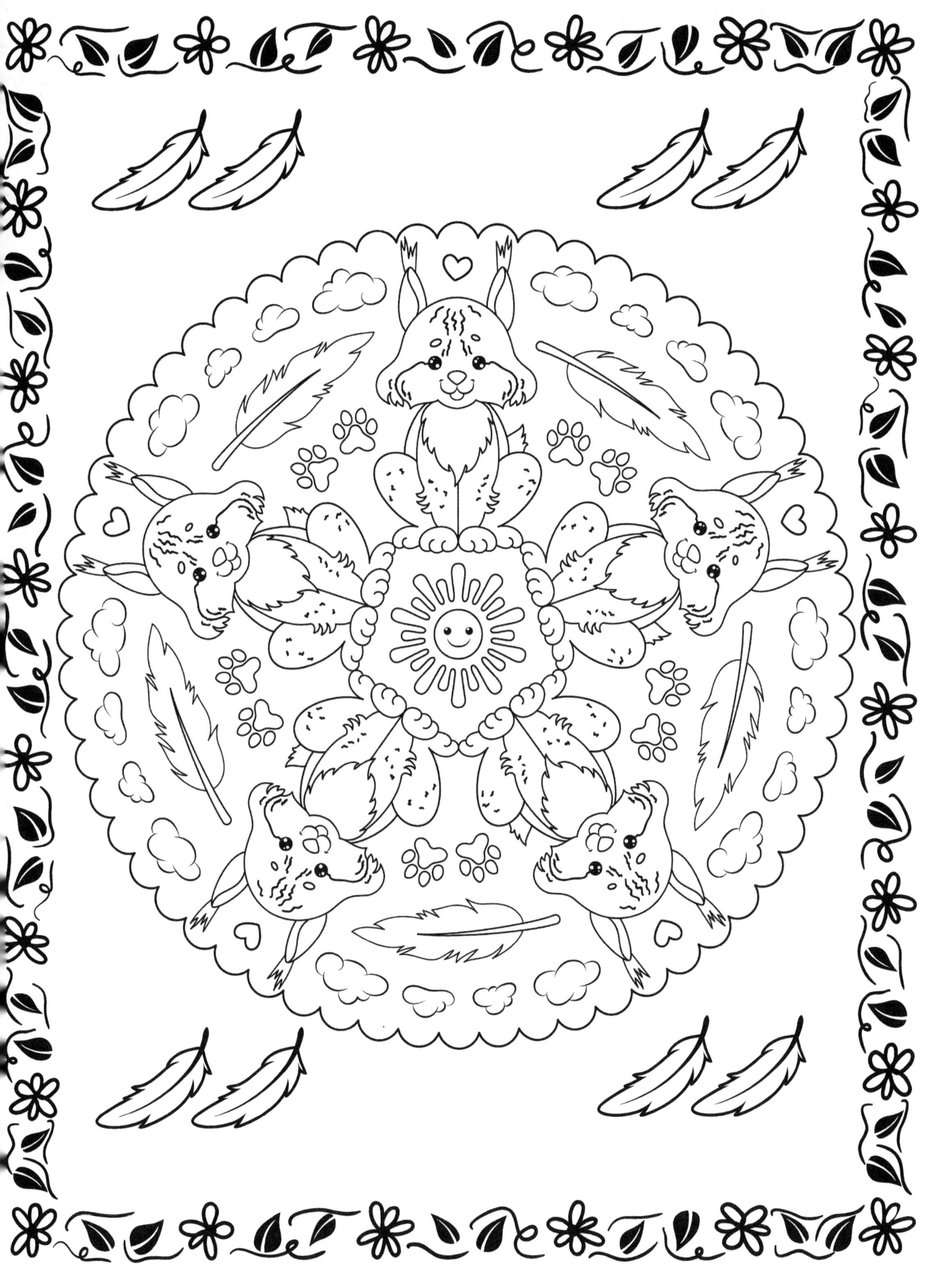

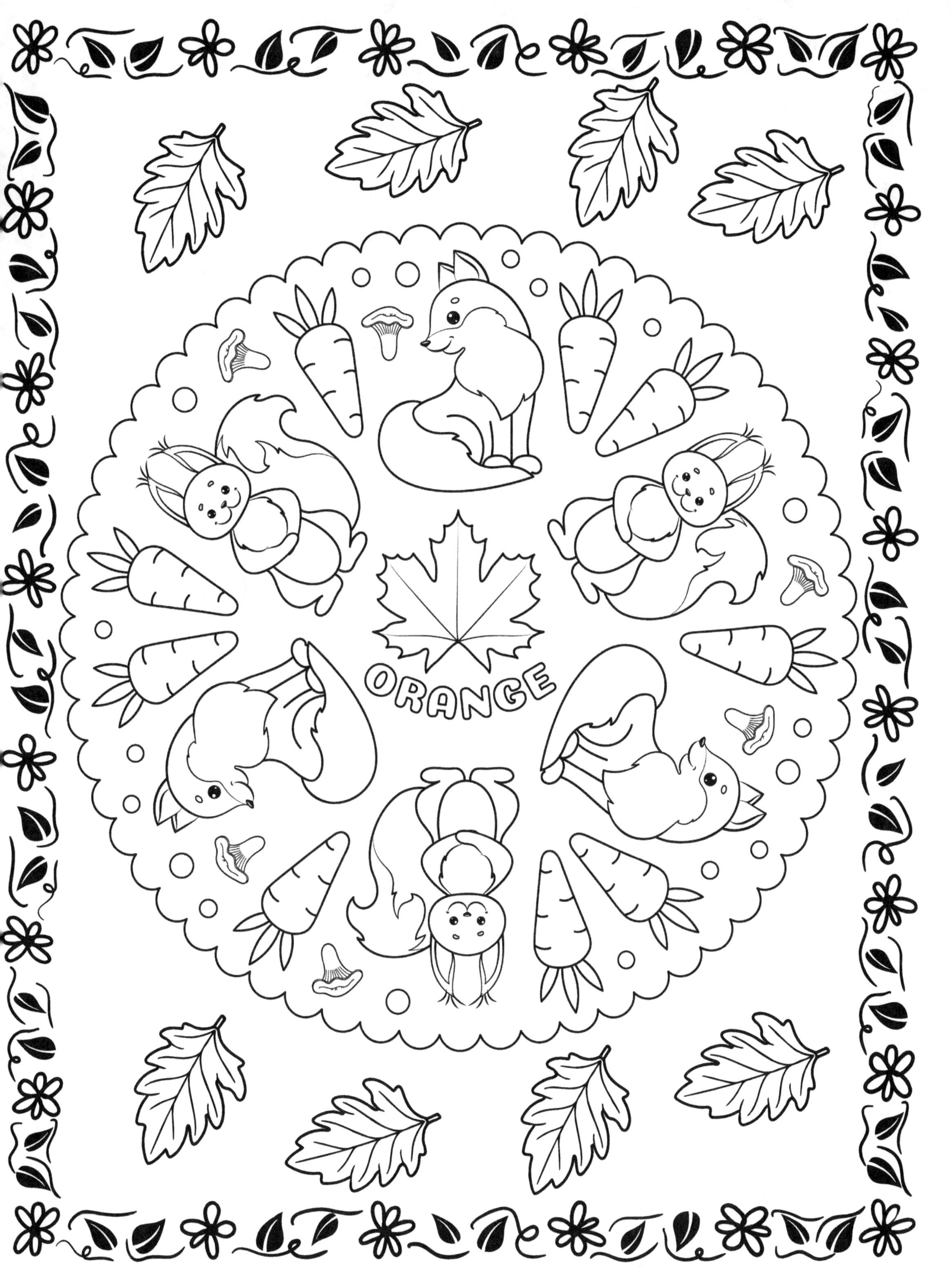
ORANGE

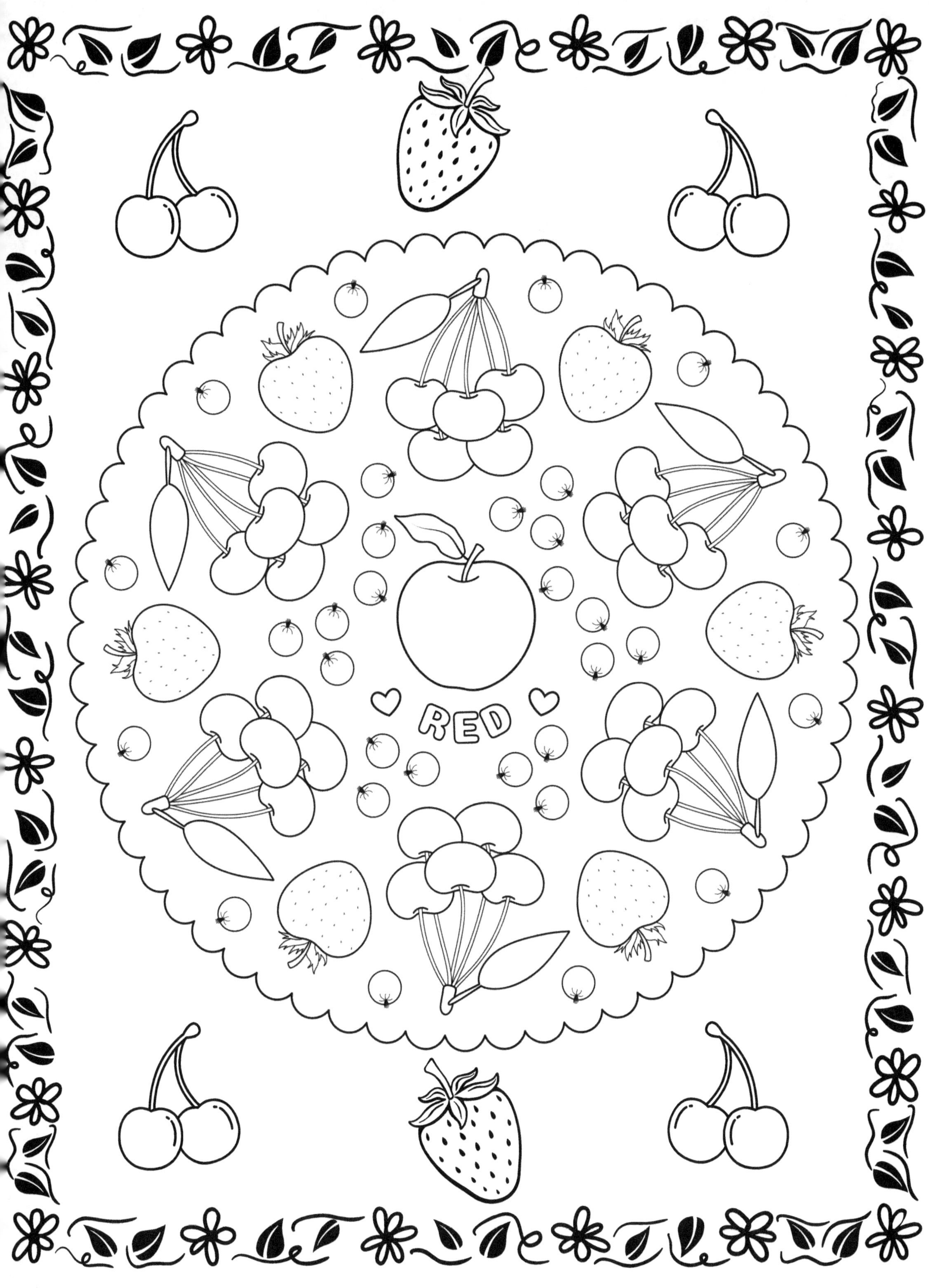

RED

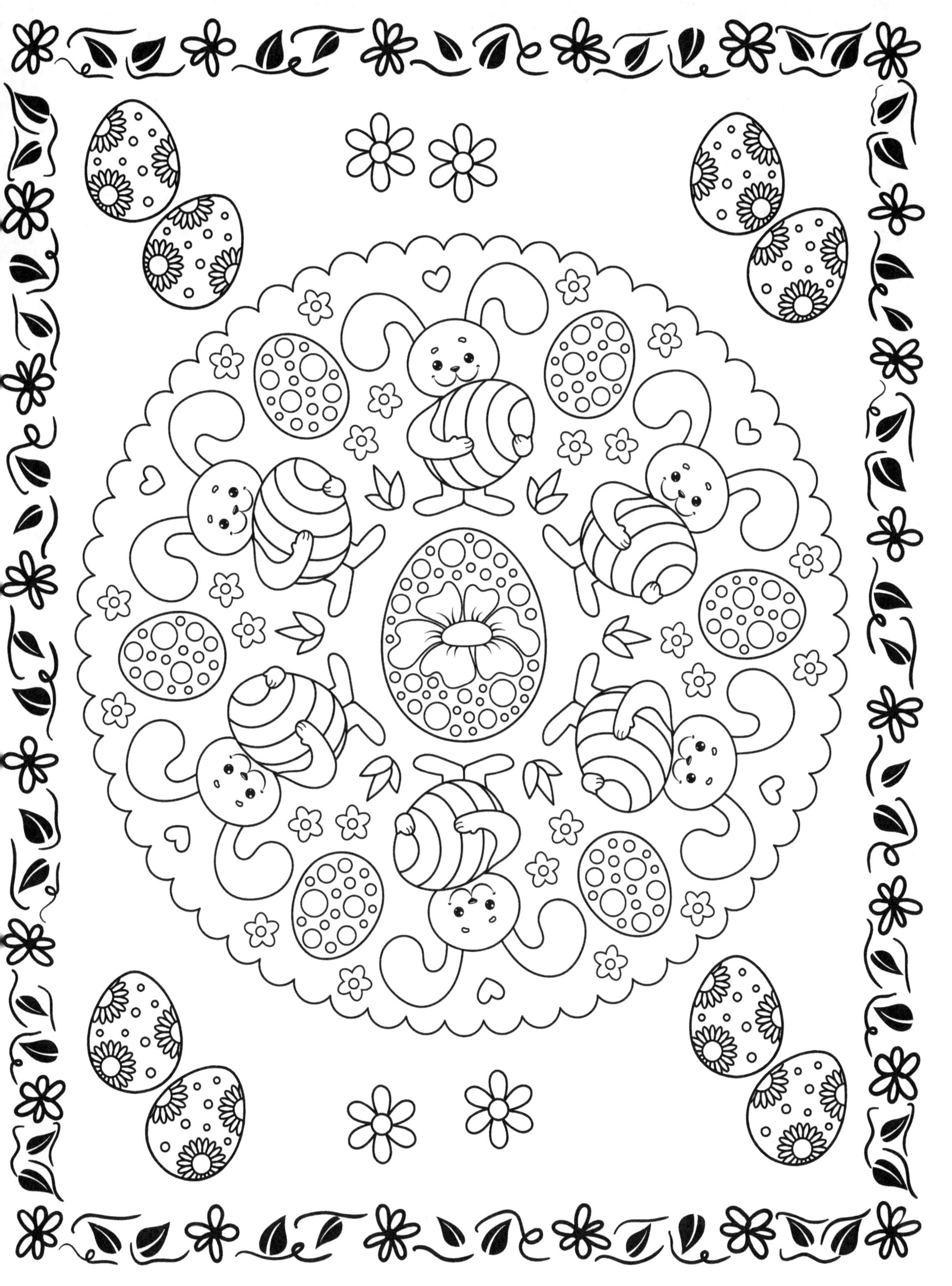

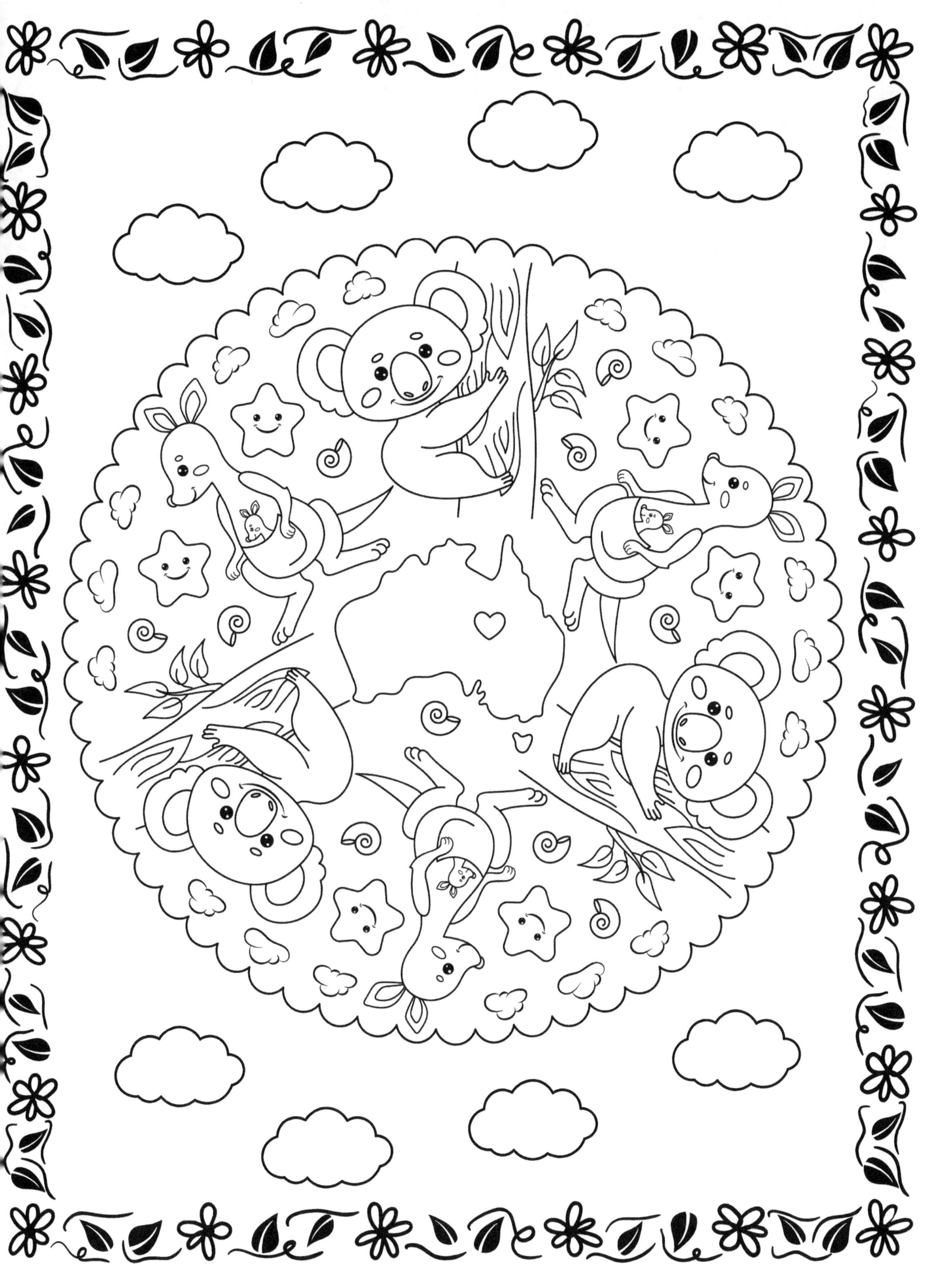

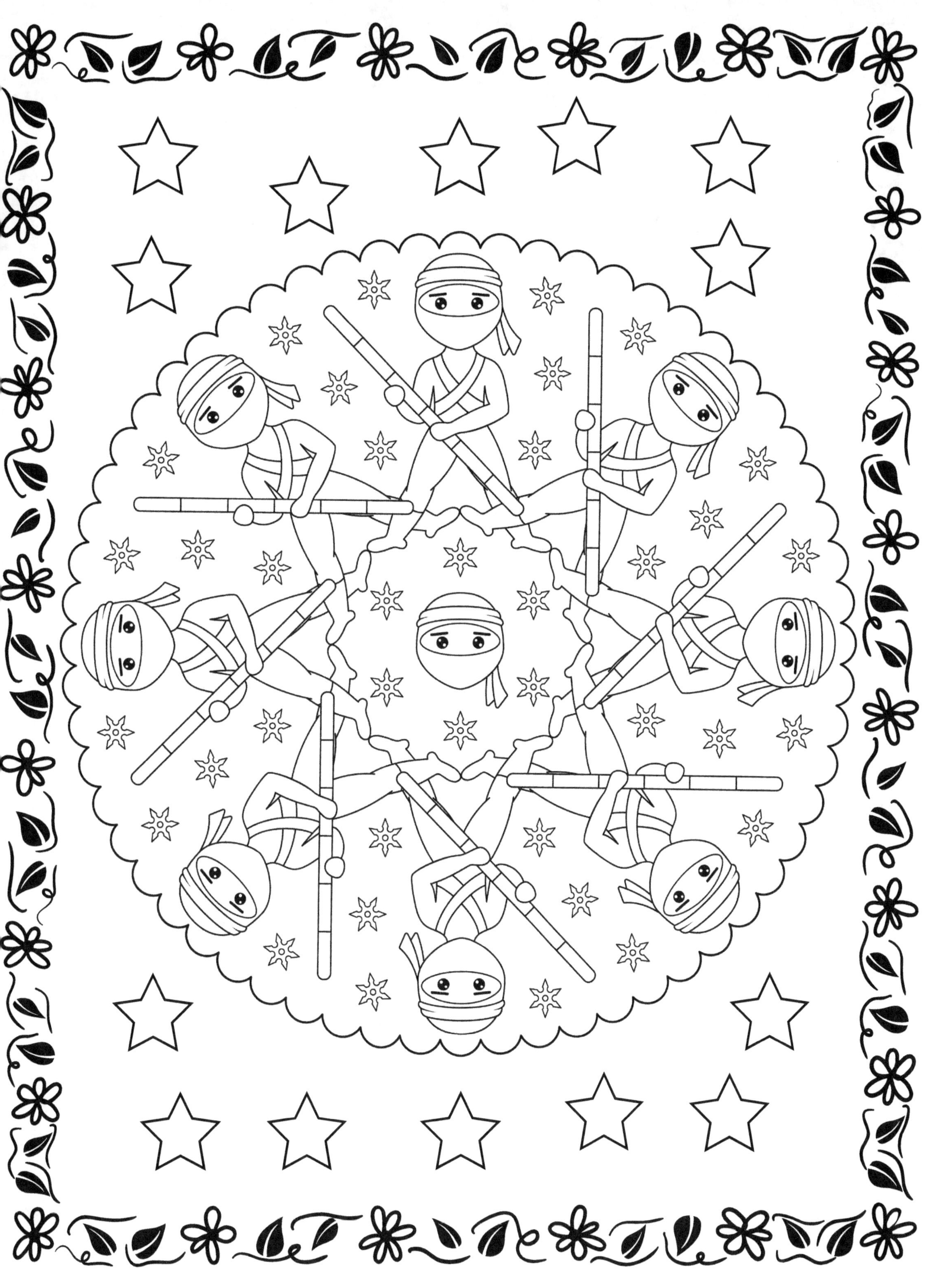

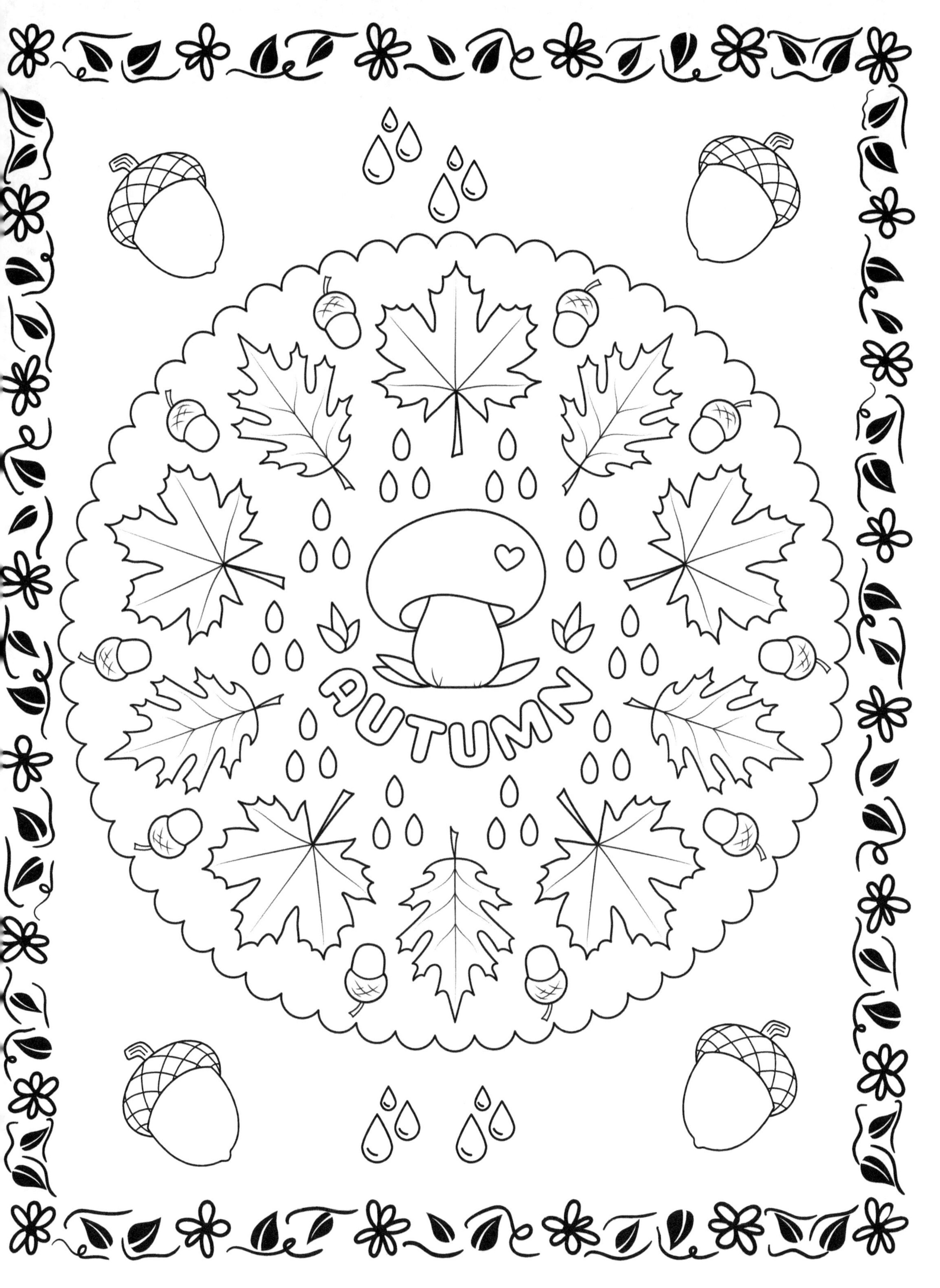

AUTUMN

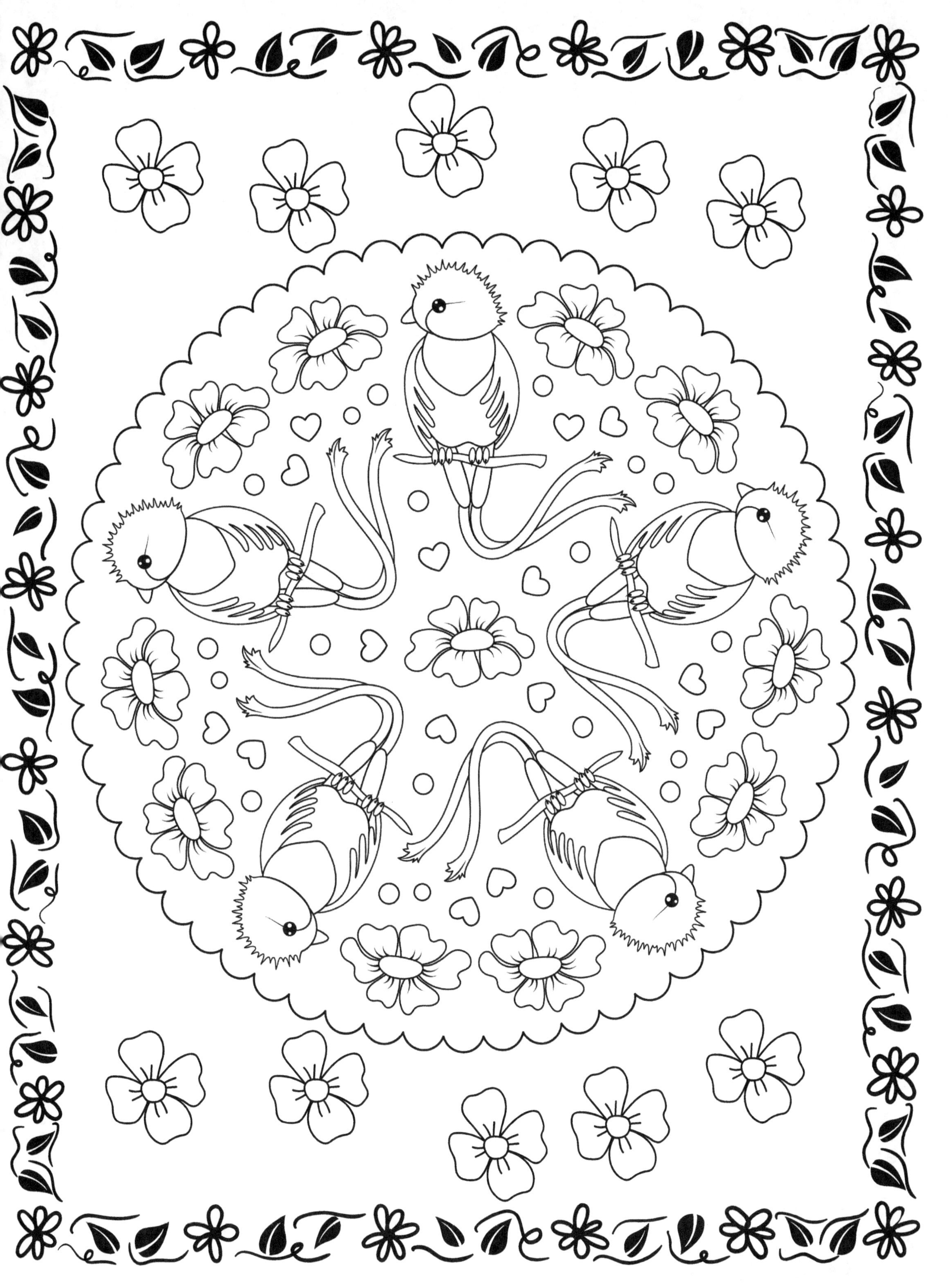